THE TRUTH
ABOUT AMAZING
KIDS

THE TRUTH

ABOUT AMAZING

KIDS

A SIMPLE GUIDE TO TRANSFORMING YOUR CHILD'S LIFE OVERNIGHT

CHRISTINE RICH HANSON

This edition published in 2012 by BTB Publishing, US.
ISBN 978-0-9857303-0-7

Library of Congress Control Number: 2012914465

Typesetting by *www.wordzworth.com*
Cover Design by *Afaheem Solutions and Steve Warwick*

BTB

BTB Publishing
1402 Regency Dr West
Savoy, IL 61874

www.ChristineRichHanson.com

ACKNOWLEDGMENTS

I thank every single person who has impacted my life in any tiny way. I needed each of the lessons.

Thank you to my terrific editor Cheryl Lehman, wikibrain Steve Warwick, all of my students and their parents, and children everywhere young and old.

Most of all thank you to JRP and Barry Orms for the gift of real Love.

To B2.0 for shining the Light, holding the depth, and showing me the Infinity of this parenthesis.

CONTENTS

FOREWORD

There is nothing easy about child rearing. There is no real road map, and no perfect template for success. Each child brings his or her own unique personality and way of understanding the world regardless of their parents' genetics or best wishes. And each next child creates a brand new family no matter how hard the parents try to establish some semblance of order, consistency, and structure.

Intensive research in many fields including: psychology; psychiatry; neuroscience; sociology and more, all continue to explore the mysteries involved in becoming, sustaining, and flourishing as a family. Each field uses different paradigms and perspective hoping to help people understand what is "really" going on through the various stages of life and human development. And, to this day, no single theory commands or dominates the field making it any easier for parents, teachers, clergy, therapists, or dance instructors to know (with certainty) that the decisions invoked are really the "right" ones insuring the best possible strategy for raising an enthusiastic, positive, and outstanding individual. Much of the work of raising children, actually, is catch-as-catch can with the majority of people seeming to share the notion that, at the very least, they want to raise a child or children differently (and better) than the way they had been brought up.

I have seen this foundational dilemma played out over and over throughout my career as a clinician, educator, consultant, and pioneer in a program designed for Grandfathers-Fathers- and Children. I have struggled with, ached, and on many occasions celebrated as my clients and students have attempted to understand marriage and family dynamics bringing new intent, focus, and purpose to the trajectory of their life experience and personal goals.

In my own work, I have come to know the interaction between parents and children as best characterized in the notion of "intimate conversations." In a real sense, all conversations with our children are intimate and model sensitivity and even passion when we, as parents, choose to slow ourselves down to truly listen and engage with the child. Truly, not all conversations with children deal, directly, with what it takes to become an "amazing" and fulfilled individual. Yet, all of our conversations support the context necessary to allow children to feel safe with their curiosity such that they can wonder out loud and with us as they engage in developing their skills and prowess through experimentation across the lifespan. The salient issue in terms of engaging a child in "dialogue" is establishing the foundation of support indicating "it is okay for you to wonder and ask, and I will take the time to listen, clarify and respond." This "meta-" message is critical for the most meaningful conversations which can and will follow as the child develops through the trials and tribulations of pre-school, the school age years, and on into puberty, young adult and finally adult life.

Facilitating "amazing" children requires parents to be "on the same page." I have yet to find a theory of marriage and family which, at one point or another, does not recognize the fundamental and critical role of the parental dyad. Without a good, solid communication base between mother and father, there is very little chance of ever establishing solid rapport with a child on any subject, let alone one as sensitive and significant as the child's emerging into his or her own sense of excellence.

Wouldn't it be great if "getting on the same page" was as easy as writing those words. It isn't. The process for being "united" requires each parent to step into awareness with a commitment to self understanding, appreciation for generational patterns (knowledge of at least 3 generations), co-equal sensitivity to one's partner, and most assuredly a commitment to genuine dialogue.

In this spirit, I was delighted when Christine Rich Hanson asked me to write the forward to her book. I remembered her work as an undergraduate student at Antioch University in Los Angeles. I recalled her wide-eyed and rapt attention in Contemporary Modes of Counseling and vividly recall her heartfelt reactions when we visited Metropolitan State Hospital. Even then it was clear, Ms. Rich was a passionate, determined, and intensely creative individual committed to the notion that "there must be a better way."

And now, she has found that "better way" articulating and integrating her sensitivity, compassion, artistry, and clinical acumen. Her refreshingly clear and straightforward commentary brilliantly draws off of her years of education, training, and personal experience. Ms. Rich Hanson is an artist fully cognizant of how dance is a metaphor for life. She knows there is no way to help a child to become "amazing" (in any field, let alone as a dancer) unless that child is supported by family and friends. And, she has been able to derive a distinctly accessible and workable methodology helping people find their way in their best effort to be astounding child facilitators, advocates, and ultimately reliable parents.

Her book reflects her courage and conviction to bring light to a shadowy area and allows us all to have, work with, and master "the moves" requisite to facilitating our children in becoming brilliant dancers as they shine as healthy and robust individuals.

Jeffrey Marsh, Ph.D.

Former Adjunct Associate Professor at University of Southern California, Department of Counseling Psychology (graduate level)

Founder of Grandfather-Father-Child Program at Stephen S. Wise Parenting Center, Los Angeles

Clinician in private practice,
Beverly Hills, California 2012

PREFACE

People have told me over and over through the years at the dance studio, "You should write a book." I always just laughed; I had never written anything more than a bit of fiction in fifth grade and some papers in college. I did take lots, and I mean lots of notes through the decades about the relationships I saw between dance students, their parents and me. Then, during the winter of 2011, I had this recurring notion: *Write a book.* I tried to push that thought aside, as I was busy choreographing, teaching, and life coaching children and parents, but the book idea kept coming back to me. I knew what I was passionate about: children, dance, and parent-child relations. So after many false starts, I began writing in earnest in January of 2012. Two months later, I had a book. It had literally poured out of me.

I have always had an affinity for children; I understand them, and they appreciate that. When I was a child, young kids always gravitated to me at family gatherings, and this continued even when I was an adult. When I became an aunt, my nieces and nephews flocked to me, and we would find creative things to do together.

This ability has developed over the years into a strong intuitive perception to understand children, even babies. Recently, I visited a friend with a two-and-a-half-month-old, and the baby and I chatted it up. I read him books and showed him toys, and he was actively engaged for an extended time. His mother said she'd never witnessed such behavior with him.

This connection I have with children is instrumental in my dance studio--sometimes in the classroom, but even more often in the hallways. I can often figure children out faster than they or their parents can. I haven't always made use of this ability; like many studio owners, I used to get impacted by the parent's issues and just hope I'd never have to deal with parents, let alone see or talk to them. It took me away from working with the children. But over the years, I have learned how to best inspire children, and facilitating better relationships with their parents is really a key to it all.

As a dance teacher, I have the honor of training dancers from toddlerhood to college. This gives me a unique advantage over academic teachers, for example, because I get to watch kids develop over the years, both as dancers and as people. I also observe their parents. I have grown to realize that the parents are really just "big kids," suffering from damage inflicted upon them by *their* parents, and unintentionally passing that damage on to their own kids. Now, instead of avoiding parents, I offer life coaching for both them and their children.

I have been a parent, and I was not perfect. Dealing with children has always been easy for me, but being a parent is a whole different story. My daughter thinks I did a wonderful job, but I see things that could have been improved upon. For example, an early divorce from her father sent me into a typical "choose me instead of him" sort of battle that did not serve any of us. I know what it's like to wonder if you're doing the right thing for your child. I know that it's that uncertainty that makes parenting so difficult. And that's why I'm writing this book: I wish I had had this kind of parenting manual when *I* needed it.

Now, as a grandparent, I have had the luxury of spending time with my grandson during his formative years. Now, I allow my intuitive self to lead the way in my interactions with him, as I have done with my dance kids. I began to realize that I was following a pattern in my dealings with children, and one day, I decided to write down the approach that I'd honed over the years. That method became the backbone of this book: the Hanson Parenting Method. I know that this method works from the point of view of a grandparent, from my dealings with my grandson. I know it works with children at the dance studio, which is like a second home to them. And I know that it works for parents, because the parents I've coached who have implemented the Hanson Parenting Method have reported back on its unmitigated success.

Across the country, I have seen the damage done to children by ill-prepared parents. I have seen the advent of more and stronger prescription drugs to alter the behavior of children, when it's really their *parents* who are scarred and ineffective, doing unintentional damage. What I see is one big cyclical mess, and I feel I have a voice to facilitate a revolutionary change.

Christine

INTRODUCTION
HELP IS ON THE WAY

Have you ever looked high and low for your glasses, only to discover they were on your head? Or searched the house for keys that were in your pocket the whole time? And where do the mates for all those lone socks go, anyway?

These are the great mysteries of the world.

What about the stuff that you know is hard, but in your most philosophical moments (Facebooking with a glass of wine), you wonder why it's so difficult at all? Like bowling, or coordinating shirts with ties. Or marriage. Or parenting—always trying to make the right choices so you don't scar your kids for life. You love your kids so much … but sometimes, being a mom or a dad is a daunting task.

Well, I have bad news, and I have good news.

I can't help you with your mate (or your socks' mates, for that matter), but I can help you parent your dancer.

And it's not as hard as you think. But it is as important as you think.

As a successful dance studio owner, teacher, choreographer, and grandparent, I know that *your* parenting can make or break any child, especially in dance. Dance requires a student to be everything on stage: a technician, an emotive actor, a performer, and an athlete, with enough courage to share all of that with an audience. To become a standout in dance, a child has to have an amazing dance teacher *and* parent. The dance teacher cannot do it alone.

After nearly three decades of teaching thousands of children dance, from toddler-beginner to stunning pre-professional, to kids who didn't speak English—or didn't speak at all, kids diagnosed with ADD, and kids who had been kicked out of 5 academic preschools -- and I've worked with their parents, I have always been curious about how to improve parent-child-studio dynamics, and I started taking notes from the beginning. As my notebooks grew and grew, I realized that there were patterns evolving which helped me understand parents and children. I can now figure kids out quickly, short-circuit even the worst meltdown, and get kids to surprise both their parents and themselves on a daily basis. My dance kids are high achievers, accomplished in dance, and earning fantastic grades. I want to teach you everything I know, so settle in and read to the end. And don't forget to share this with your child's other parent—your child needs everyone on board to support him[1] to amazingness.

---

[1]   In an effort to represent kids of both genders, I alternate between "he" and "she" throughout the book.

CHAPTER ONE

THE HANSON PARENTING METHOD™

Bad parenting has become the elephant in our collective living room. We see bad parenting all the time—in stores, in front of the daycare center, at Little League events and in our homes. We've heard the yelling and the outbursts; we've seen the violence. But no one wants to discuss it. There's the mentality that children can deal with whatever it is you're bringing. They can't. Their scars deepen over time.

Children are like fresh clay. They want to grow and learn, and they are attuned to detail. In dance, we take advantage of that ability by asking students to pay attention to the turnout of their feet; the position of their fingers, their necks, their shoulders; how they style their hair; and what they wear. Such details make the difference between a mediocre dancer and a fantastic one.

Children's attention to detail also means that they internalize all the actions of their parents.

> *We need to teach them our best attributes rather than our worst; to do so, we have to open our brains and hearts to what we are doing as parents.*

Put a microscope on it.

We rarely see great parenting. Parenting as many of us know it now is the product of generations of misdirection; it has become so inbred that it is a deformed, ugly mess. Yet we still try to puff air into it and use it despite all of its gross incompetencies.

It's time for a new model. It's time for the Hanson Method.

The Hanson Parenting Method is rooted in three Core Principles, which I describe in detail below. Based on these Core Principles, I have three tools for dealing with problematic behavior: the mainstay of my method—the Six Steps to Sanity™—which is described at the end of this chapter, and two other techniques: the Two-Way Time Out™ and the Quick Reprimand™, which are described in Chapter 5. You will be able to use these simple techniques to eradicate chaos, arguments, negative talk, and general parenting ineffectiveness. You will find that you and your child are so much more confident and happy, that waking up every day will be a joy.

Sometimes you just need someone to help you. I will.

Let's start.

CORE PRINCIPLE 1:
PARENTING WHILE AWAKE

Many parents are asleep on the job. Whether it's because they're relying on parenting the way they were parented, or because they're falling back on some commonly accepted (but unacceptable) stereotypical responses to children, they need to wake up and really *think* about what they're doing.

YOU ARE NOT YOUR PARENT

The biggest addiction in our society is not what you would expect. It's not drugs, sex, or rock 'n' roll for parents. It's parenting ineffectively just as our parents did. Oh, you may think that you are the polar opposite of your parents, but at the root, your emotional dysfunction will rear its ugly head and wreak havoc which is the same thing that your parents did to you. The longer we are allowed to engage this way, the more addicted to that behavior we become. It's the great addiction of our times that nobody speaks of.

Only with conscious action can you break the ties that harm you— and your child.

Even if you think you were raised by or are acting like Mother Theresa and Buddha themselves, question how you are engaging as a parent. Apply critical thinking.

Comfort in the Familiar

Sometimes we choose to follow our parents' model because it's familiar. It feels safe—we've been down that path and know it well. "I know it well" translates in our brains to "it is safe." We want our kids to be safe, so we push our experiences onto them.

Adopting this mindset often leads parents to try to turn their child into a mini-me. A firefighter might have a son who wants to be a dancer; the father pictures his son broke and wasting away in the bowels of a New York theater. Meanwhile, the dad is running into houses on fire. He trusts himself—he trusts what he knows. So he pushes his son to become a firefighter.

Career choice is just one example; others may sound like, "All of us Monroes go to Junction College," "We drive German-made cars," or "Baseball is the only real sport—that's what your father played." This mini-me attitude extends all the way from "We say 'Sir' and 'Ma'am'" to "If we have an argument with each other, we yell and scream," and "Go outside to get the switch I'm going to whip you with."

People often just do things the same way their parents did without any critical examination, without any *effort* to be the best at the one thing they should be getting right: parenting their own children.

Fear of Change

And then there are those who realize their parents did a poor job, yet they don't do any better, despite their desire to do so. Desire is not enough. If desire were all that we needed to grant our wishes, we would all be with People magazine's Sexiest Person, lunching with the great brains of our times, wearing our ideal sizes, and living in our dream houses.

> *Desire and intention are all well and good, but it takes action to effect change.*

There are all kinds of reasons and excuses for not taking action. Many adults fear failure. What if you put yourself out there and then feel like a fool if it doesn't work out like you'd planned? Or maybe success is really what you're afraid of. What would happen to you if you were successful? Maybe you fear your parents rejecting you for not parenting the way they did, or you think the effort to make the change to better parenting would be too exhausting.

When you stop and think about it, why does our society not encourage us to train to be parents? In dance, people can twirl around their own homes, freestyle at social gatherings, or play *Dance Party 3* on the Wii all they want, but it's never going to get them through professional choreography or a pas de deux. In order to be a *great* dancer, you have to take ballet, tap, and jazz dance very seriously. Dance is an art form to be studied and mastered through repetition.

Being a parent is one of the greatest, most important things you will ever do. Isn't it arrogant, then, that so many adults assume that having a child automatically qualifies them to be good parents? To be a healthy, respectful, and effective parent, you need to study. You need to train. And you need to throw away any prior notions you have about how children should be raised, and start fresh.

Even the word "parenting" has become bogged down, associated with practices that have no place in your home.

> *To help wipe your mind clean of all your prior parenting experience, I want you to think of yourself as a Child Facilitator.*

Facilitating your child's growth to independence and adulthood is devoid of scarring for both of you. Create structure, give encouragement, and provide a safe environment for learning and self-discovery for these exceptional beings who are your children.

DO NOT FALL FOR SOCIETAL STEREOTYPES

When we reach for a stereotyped expression, a one-size-fits-all Band-Aid to avoid dealing with children at a respectful level, we are reaching into a medicine kit of topical agents handed down in society to quickly but ineffectively numb children.

Falling Down and Flying Over

During an observation class, with 20 families gathered to watch their kids, a six-year-old girl named Mandy[2] ran to do a grand jeté leap, and she tripped over an object that she normally clears easily. She ran to her mom, who smothered her in kisses, but she continued to sob loudly.

I was concerned about what was going on with Mandy, since her mom's kisses weren't abating the near-hyperventilation and sobbing. I called Mandy over to me, and as she approached, I consciously slowed myself way down and breathed deeply, so I

---

[2]   All of the stories used as examples in this book are true, but I have changed the names to protect the identities of the children.

could be calm while I was talking to her. I crouched down to her eye level, and I turned my body to protect her from all the other parents and students.

The logical assumption was that she was crying because she'd fallen so hard, but if you rely on assumptions, you often miss the real problem, so I dismissed that thought and whispered, so that she would have to stop crying to hear me, "Hey, Mandy I'm sorry you fell. I bet that you are really upset because you usually fly over that bucket."

She nodded. With that affirmation from her, I continued, "And I bet you want everyone to know that, don't you?"

She nodded vigorously.

I said, "Do you want to go try it again?"

She didn't answer in words, but she ran back to the starting line, and through tears, she ran and FLEW over the bucket, clearing it by 2½ feet. The parents erupted in applause, but I silenced them with a wave of my hand. The clapping was a stereotyped response that would confuse Mandy. Why should she get applause for doing what 18 other kids had done? No one else got applause. The other kids think, "Hey, I didn't get any applause, and now my mom is clapping for this kid who had a meltdown?"

My conversation with Mandy restored her bruised pride, because I didn't assume to know what was wrong with her—I *asked*. This is a key step in my Six Steps to Sanity, which I will explain in detail at the end of this chapter. As it turned out, Mandy had not been crying because she was physically hurt. Kisses (or bribing, or ranting, or glaring) do not address the causes of a meltdown, but these are typical reactions of parents everywhere. What Mandy really needed was the acknowledgment that she was capable. When she got that, she was able to reset and calm down. So don't rely on the old standbys. Stay in the moment and listen to what your child has to say.

Do you see how as a society we reach for these stock responses but never stop to fully THINK about the impact on the child? I'm not naïve enough to think that the parents weren't celebrating

Mandy's get-back-up-on-the-horse spirit, *wishing they too could be that courageous*. But I always say the adults have to guide the children first, and help themselves second.

A boy falls, and even before assessing the situation, we say "You're okay. Get up." If a girl falls, we coddle her and kiss her boo-boos. And the list goes on—in this next story alone, you'll see seven stereotypical behaviors that adults often fall into when dealing with children.

Circles of Life: A Symphony of Stereotypes in 7 parts

I was invited to a birthday dinner in a private room of a restaurant. Four different ethnicities were represented, but the stereotyping in this story was simply something parents at large do—it was not cultural.

We had a rather large group, consisting of about half children and half adults, and the parents were discussing how to arrange the tables. As inevitably happens, all the kids were assigned to one table, and the adults to the other. One mother said, "Yes, let's put them over there, so we don't have to deal with them. We deal with them all the time." This is:

Societal Stereotype #1: Sequestering the children to their own table, implying that they are boring or draining.

(It also makes no sense, practically speaking. Just because they are thrown together does not mean they can all suddenly fend for themselves without parental assistance. I always laugh when this happens, because not having your young child next to you requires you to get up from your meal to go help them out with various meal-time issues.)

They could have easily made one huge table, with all of us together. We were there to celebrate one of the *children's* birthdays! But they separated us, as though something great was going to happen amongst the adults. Interestingly, as the night continued, the conversation at the adult table revolved around the mundane topics of food, weather, and work, while at the kids' table, the five-year-old was entertaining the teens with her antics. I always say the kids have a wealth of smarts and entertainment to be inspired by.

After we had all seated ourselves at our designated tables, the food began to come out. The adults at the grown-up table didn't notice what was going on at the children's table, but I saw that there were still two kids waiting patiently for their food—a teen and the five-year-old. Soon, the waitress arrived with a peanut butter and jelly sandwich and gave it to the five-year-old, assuming it was hers.

The five-year-old looked at the sandwich in front of her, probably thinking, *Wait I ordered a salad.*

The teen gracefully said the sandwich was hers.

The five-year-old, who still had nothing to eat, said, "Where's mine?" which finally prompted a response from the adults over in their own world.

Two of the adults turned around and assumed the PBJ was for the five year old—which meant the teen had to explain—again—that it was hers. This is:

Societal Stereotype #2: Foodism.

We think PBJ is a kid thing; that's why it was served to the five-year-old, causing embarrassment to the teen. But even adults like PBJ and mac 'n' cheese. Why do we have to assume they're for kids? Conversely, foodism would have us believe a salad is too grown up for a five-year-old, as though she can't have the palate of an older person. Don't we want our kids to eat vegetables?

Then the five-year-old's parents explained to her that the PBJ belonged to the teen—as though the five-year-old had been responsible for the mix-up and was poised to dive into the PBJ at any minute. The five-year-old, who already knew who the PBJ belonged to, began to pout. And this is:

Societal Stereotype #3: Assuming a five-year-old will grab whatever is in front of her. Give her some credit. She's not a dog.

The five-year-old's Caver parents made the wrong assumption about her pout, thinking it was due to not having any food. They started in with the "Oh, honey, your food is coming," which nudged the pout toward a blow up.

Societal Stereotype #4: A young child has to be served first, or she will act out.

If the parents had moved past this stereotype and just *asked* their child what was going on, she could have told them.

I summoned the five-year-old, and she came over, still pouty.

I whispered, "I bet you're actually upset that everyone thought that you had done something bad because the waitress put the PBJ sandwich in front of you. They were all talking like you had taken her sandwich, right?"

She nodded, relieved to be understood. I continued, "The waitress just made a mistake. The adults weren't paying attention. I know that you weren't trying to take the sandwich."

The pout went away, and she returned to her seat.

Soon, her salad came, and she started to eat, but she needed help cutting something, so she went to her mom for assistance. The mom went to the child's seat to cut her food.

About four minutes later, something happened, and all of a sudden, the five-year-old was acting like a two-year-old, crying and straddling her mom's lap, while her mother hugged her and rocked her. The child was repeatedly saying, "No!" to her mom, and sort of slapping her mom for emphasis. Five-year-olds do not behave like that unless their parents allow them to. The dad made no move, and the mom kept trying to baby the child and stroke her hair, fanning the flames of the temper tantrum, which was only growing louder.

It was hard to ignore, although everyone was trying to. This was...

Societal Stereotype #5: ignoring a child's meltdown when a parent has lost control of the situation.

Society tells us the only thing we can do is let the parent handle it. This often entails an irate parent making a scene and brutally punishing the child on the spot, or a helpless parent letting the child make the scene, because the parent doesn't know what to do. Either way, everyone suffers together.

I got up and asked the mom what the problem was.

She said, "The real problem, or what she thinks the problem is?"

I said, "Either way, let's hear it."

"She thinks she doesn't have any ketchup, but it's right here," she said, indicating the container of ketchup. Continuing as though the child couldn't hear or understand English, she said, "I think she's just tired."

The child squirmed in her mother's lap, her face burrowed into the mom's chest, repeating, "No! No!"

Now the mom was guilty of:

Societal Stereotype #6: talking about the child to another adult in front of the child, as though the child doesn't know what's going on.

They can hear you. Show some respect.

I said, "Does she still nap in the afternoon?" It was 5:00 p.m.

"No, she hasn't napped since she was two." Clearly, this five-year-old wasn't tired, despite what her mother had said. The ketchup was not the issue, either. I suspected the child's issue was a combination of her parents' dynamics with her, coupled with the fact that her mom had not acknowledged her daughter's being publicly humiliated by the misplacement of the PBJ sandwich. This was not the time or place for the Six Steps to Sanity, with her mother right there contributing to the meltdown, so I went with the Quick Reprimand for both of them—a technique I will discuss in detail later.

I said firmly to the five-year-old, "You have to stop. We're at a gathering, and you do not carry on like this. Here are your choices. If you are very tired, like your mom thinks, then you need to excuse yourself and go home and take a nap. Otherwise, if you stay here, you have to eat peacefully like everyone else. It's your choice."

I got up and went back to my seat, putting my finger to my mouth to silently shush the mother, lest she continue to baby the child and make it worse.

The child's tears stopped, and she went back to her meal. *Everyone else thought the Red Sea had parted, but I had just used the Hanson Method.*

Ten minutes later, the five-year-old was entertaining the teens and dancing with her doll, unintentionally displaying her flexibility, a result of her hard work in dance class. Another mother asked who her dance teachers were and how long she had been training, and then she remarked, "Wow, she was just born that way."

Huh? What were the teachers and the dance class for? Eating pizza?!

Societal Stereotype #7 is downplaying our children's efforts.

No child is born with his feet turned out for ballet. They have to work at it. The same goes for great swimmers, runners, painters, pianists, etc. Acknowledge that. Don't dismiss their efforts with a comment like "He was born like that."

Do you see how one casual gathering with adults and children together was loaded down with seven stereotypes? No one was doing it to the adults. Just to the kids. *These stereotypes disrespect children, and they're not okay, even if everyone else engages in such behavior.* The children didn't do this kind of stuff. I often think,

"Who are the people acting like adults in the room?" And they're usually sitting at the kids' table.

IT'S TIME TO WAKE UP

I've just dismissed many of the every-body-else-did-them knee-jerk reactions, so you may be sitting there wondering what the heck *to* do. I think that's a better place to be in. You're awake. You're in the moment.

At teachingsofthebuddha.com, I found one of my favorite stories:

It is said that soon after his enlightenment, the Buddha passed a man on the road who was struck by the Buddha's extraordinary radiance and peaceful presence.
The man stopped and asked, "My friend, what are you? Are you a celestial being or a god?"
"No," said the Buddha.
"Well, then, are you some kind of magician or wizard?"
Again, the Buddha answered, "No."
"Are you a man?"
"No."
"Well, my friend, then what are you?"
The Buddha replied, "I am awake."

Whether you practice or study spirituality or not, the message is a good one. Being awake requires you to be in this moment, not yesterday's. *Staying* awake is the challenge.

Yesterday, you knew something about your child. Today, she is a different person.

If you consistently see her as yesterday's child and apply one-size-fits-all parenting riffs to your child today, you will be laying the foundation for problems.

At which point do you give her credit for being older? When her school picture comes out? When she enters a new grade? At her wedding?

Hard as it is, wake up every day and think of your child as a new person. Your child learned something yesterday, so he is different. Today. You are different, too. Being awake to this moment and your child keeps things fresh.

Being awake keeps you aware of a child's needs right now. My "Circles of Life" story above shows just how asleep we adults are. We make assumptions and play it safe, avoiding critical thinking and real engagement.

Things are happening to our children right before our eyes, and we are blinded by the past...

...past parenting methods, our own childhoods, events from earlier in the day—everything but this moment. We've been taught by society to sleepwalk through life.

If you have any interest in your child being amazing in dance and in life, you have to wake up.

You have to participate in the moment, educate, and communicate.

Those are the hallmarks of a parent who is awake.

Life is an improv. You have to be confident enough to figure out from moment to moment what is required of you as the parent to most effectively deal with your child. If you sleepwalk through your parenting, how are you going to see the things affecting your child?

CORE PRINCIPLE 2:
PARENTING A CHILD, NOT A PRISONER

Children are people. Not prisoners to punish, to treat as criminals, to order around and then ignore. Not dolls, nuisances, headaches, objects owned, three-dimensional DNA, something-I-created-on-a-date, offspring, clients, anesthetic for the pain of life, or little tests of your abilities. People. People with brains, hearts, dreams, and challenges. People who need to be loved, encouraged, respected, engaged, and more. This core concept—or lack thereof—jams parents up 100% of the time.

Objectifying our children—thinking of them as less than people—is a common trap that we adults fall into. And the result? Hell on earth. Objectified children will rebel—as they should! Do you blame them? How would you react if someone treated you that way?

What Lasts Longer Than an Energizer Bunny?
An Upset Toddler

I was at an international ballet competition in Chicago with some of my students and teachers. It was the judges' lunch break, and I was in the theater chatting with another choreographer, when two of my teachers came running up to me, horror in their eyes.

"Christine, you have to come immediately to the women's bathroom downstairs. It's not good. There is a woman with a toddler, and that baby is going to die, he's screaming and crying so much. It's been going on the whole time we've been waiting in line for the restrooms—like 15 minutes. He won't stop, and the mother has lost it, and—just HURRY!"

We all ran out of the auditorium. As I approached the stairs, I could hear the most awful, blood-curdling screams. I imagined tooth extraction, beating—the worst. I passed a line of women waiting outside the ladies' lounge, looking like deer in headlights, and made my way through two sets of doors to witness the scene.

Toilets overflowing, hand dryers blasting heat, snow boot slush melting on the floor, and women washing their hands, alternately glaring or gaping at the train wreck at hand, over by the sinks: a mother and her 3-year-old boy in a standoff—and it wasn't a silent one.

There was no hitting or screaming from the mom, but the toddler was standing there in diapers and snow boots, screaming at the top of his lungs. His little face was beet red, and that child could wail like a tornado siren. At issue: the mom wanted him to do a poo in the toilet. The boy did not want to.

Of *course* he didn't want to. He was being made a spectacle of in a public arena. Sometimes moms and dads pick the worst times to stand up and pretend to parent—in this case, because the mom felt that her son was too old for diapers, and that the people around her would think so, too. But she wasn't thinking of her son as a person. If she had been, she wouldn't have stripped him down and publicly humiliated him. And what did she get for her trouble? Hell on earth—a hot, stinky, tiny three-stall bathroom reverberating with her child's screaming.

I walked right up to the boy, took a deep breath, calmed myself into slow motion, squatted down, smiled, and said I had a story to tell him. He stopped screaming. I took his hand and led him and his mom to an open area outside the bathroom, whipped out my cell phone, and started playing videos of my grandson doing silly things. I asked the little boy if he was hungry, and he said he was, so I asked his mom if she had any snacks. She produced some crackers, which I handed to him. While he was munching away, I put his clothes back on him, gave the mother some tips on potty training—mostly centered on the idea that people need to be relaxed to have a bowel movement. I suggested she find a quiet place for him to nap for now, as he was clearly exhausted, and then later that evening, after a meal, she could put him on the potty chair and read him his favorite books, focusing on the stories instead of the poo release.

The next day, I saw the little boy with his mom and dad at the hotel breakfast buffet. The little boy lit up when he saw me, and the mom did, too. She thanked me profusely, saying she didn't know what she would have done if I hadn't stopped to help—so many people had glared at her, and she had felt embarrassed and at a loss for what to do. And she reported that that night, the little boy had gotten on the toilet and finally did a poo, according to my suggestions.

The moral of the story? Simple. Treat your child like a human being. If you don't, you'll be sorry.

THE WAYS WE OBJECTIFY OUR KIDS

Core Principle #2 is deceptive in its simplicity. It sounds so obvious—if asked, most parents would say, "Of course my child is a person. Duh."

> But *there are subtle ways that parents objectify their kids, and they're often things your own parents did that you accept without question.*

They're socially acceptable, despite the detriment they do to kids. Check the examples below, and see if any of them sound familiar to you.

"Kids are to be seen and not heard."

Most of us assume this means the child should be "polite" and quiet when adults are talking to each other, or at a public gathering. This sends the message that it's okay for the parents to talk, but not for kids to. Somehow children don't rank high enough on the verbal value scale? Do we have to separate adults and children for conversation? How many times have you heard (or said), "We're having an adult conversation. Why don't you go play?"

With the Hanson Method, adults recognize that children might actually have something to contribute—and that it may even be wiser than what the adults have to say. Children can be taught to converse politely with adults.

If we continue to keep kids out of our conversations, there will be negative consequences.

Either the children will become attention-seekers, acting out so you can't continue your conversation, manufacturing drama to get you to look their way, wailing at the slightest provocation, etc.; or they will become so quiet and withdrawn that their participation in life will be impacted. They will become hesitant to answer questions at school, they'll shy away from engaging in conversations with friends, or they'll be afraid to ask for help from adults when they need it.

I have witnessed the effects of children objectified as a result of the "seen and not heard" mindset. For example, in dance class, these same children will be unable to ask to go to the bathroom and just go right there in class. They will be so unsure of themselves that it is too overwhelming to answer the easiest dance terminology question. On the other end of the spectrum, some young children who are always shushed come to class and see it as an opportunity to catch up. They want to share about their upcoming play dates, their trip to grandma's, their parents' ages, and what happened at their parents' doctor appointments.

You may have to be very patient waiting for your young one to share their verbal contribution, but a parent's inability to do this is tied to being more worried about the other adult and what they think. It could also be a failure to slow down when alone with the child.

It's best to stop, take the time, and recognize that your child has something interesting to say.

I learn something every day from kids.

"I'm the parent, so you'd better respect me."

This idea comes from a variety of cultural models, but let's skip the analysis of its origin and think of the mindset in another way. What if, at Subway, when you stepped up to order, the person preparing your food said in a pompous tone, "I'm the Sandwich Artist here at Subway. That's right. So you'd better respect me." Yeah, it doesn't really inspire deep feelings of respect, does it?

For me, respect is experienced and given freely, not demanded from the title police.

Just because you have given yourself the title of parent does not mean you are deserving of a child's respect, even if it's your own child.

Same for dance teachers. If you secretly assume that a title gets an automatic response of respect from a child, just remember the child didn't get the same contract!

This is what I love about teaching the three-year-olds: they tell it like it is. They have no sense of respect. I have to work to earn their cooperation, because if they don't like something, they just say, "I'm a little bit bored, so I'm going home." Similarly, if I tried to do all fun things, they wouldn't buy that, either. They have to have authentic balance, or they will want to walk. When I teach a room of 20 three-year-olds, I start by treating them as people and giving them value through education. They pick up on this immediately, and I've earned their respect by being consistent. Older kids, of course, have learned to filter their responses, but the way to earn respect from children—from *people,* in general—is to treat them like human beings consistently. Because that's what they are.

"My child is a prince/princess."

What about the children who come to me as princes and princesses? I'm all for treating your children well, but we can't cave in to our kids, letting them do whatever they wish and superficially propping them up with external fluffery. That is...

> ... the other end of treating them as less than human: adopting the mindset that they cannot be communicated with, but must be appeased at all costs.

I asked Larissa Saveliev, former member of Bolshoi Ballet and founder and artistic director of Youth America Grand Prix, the world's largest student ballet scholarship competition, about some of her encounters with such parenting. She said, "[One] time a wealthy father took three floors of a hotel, so his competing daughter would not be disturbed. Another father had a masseuse travel along with them and wanted a room backstage for her to be massaged. In [both] cases the dancers were not good." Indeed, treating your child like a princess does not do her any favors.

I often see the effects of this kind of objectification when it comes to our dress code at the studio. Every once in awhile, a mother will bring her preschooler to dance in something other than the plain leotard required—perhaps a lively Disney princess leotard/attached skirt/marabou feather combo, with lots of bows in the hair. I always stop such families at the classroom door and ask them where their dress code attire is, and the parents' response is often something along the lines of, "Well, Suzie didn't want to wear it. She would only wear this."

Such a parent is afraid of her own child's emotional threats, and since she doesn't see her daughter as a person but as an object—a doll that can go crazy on her at any moment—it doesn't occur to her to parent her. When the mom attempts to switch the girl to the regulation leotard, she is met with a nuclear meltdown.

At this point, I generally step in, kneel down, and say something like, "Hi, Suzie. I'm happy that you are signed up for dance class. We have a rule that all the students have to wear this plain leotard. If you want to take dance class, this is what you have to wear. Would you like to wear this so you can go to dance class?" I would say that 98% of the time, the child agrees to change. (The other 2% is when her parent interrupts, or the child is about to come down with an illness, which often causes fussiness and inability to focus.)

Dress code is one thing, but there are so many more weighty consequences of this kind of objectification, as well. I've devoted a whole section to it later in the book. (See "Caving in to Chaos," part of Chapter 7.)

"My child is my prize possession."

Some parents introduce their children with a string of accolades over and over again: "Oh, this is Johnny, who won the platinum ribbon for outstanding solo in the musical theater category at the Make-'em-A-Star dance competition. Honey, show them that one move."

Now, many parents would think this is a positive thing—giving their child positive reinforcement. But...

> ... if you lead with that stuff when introducing your children, it's as though you only value them for what they have accomplished.

You are treating them as prized possessions. As a result, they will begin to act out in one of two ways: by becoming boastful, or by becoming withdrawn out of fear that if they don't continue winning, they will not be introduced at all. Children who boast and children who are withdrawn both feel insecure, because they know they are being praised for an accomplishment while their essence is glossed over. They both hold back and never want to fully engage.

Even the Kids are Brainwashed

These are just a few of the ways that we objectify our kids, and even our children believe society's spin that these behaviors are okay.

Life sentence?

When I told a group of students aged 9 to 16 that the premise of this book was that children are born perfect, and that it's their parents' ineffectiveness that causes problems, their jaws dropped to floor, and they looked at each other like, "Did you hear that!? I've never heard anything like that! Did she really have the courage to say that?!"

I went on, "And I don't believe in spanking, yelling, grounding, or taking things away."

Their minds were blown. They kept looking at each other to check if they were hearing things correctly.

One child responded incredulously, "But if you don't do that to us how will we behave?"

Wow. Societal spin, indoctrination, or brainwashing? D: all of the above.

I said, "I don't do any of that to you, nor do I cave in to you, and you mind me all the time. I tell it like it is. I believe in a Time-Out or a Quick Reprimand."

Another child countered, "But you're our teacher, and we have a different relationship with you. And, well, yeah—we just agree with you. But our parents, we ignore them, or we—"

"It's like our parents have to show us love," interrupted another girl, "And then if we do something wrong, they have to show us the opposite, like how *mad* they are at us, so we won't do that again...right?"

I said, "Uh-uh. I think they get mad and blow up because they didn't teach you the value of why not to do something in the first place, plus they generally don't know what they're doing, and neither did their parents."

"But even if they knew what they were doing," piped up another child, "Wouldn't the parents still have to nearly kill us to get us to cooperate?"

I said, "Again, I don't have any problems with any of you. And what about my grandson? He never gets in trouble."

"Well he's smart," someone answered.

I countered, "And you're not? No, I just used my parenting techniques with him. That's the way a parent-child relationship can be."

They were all speechless.

As smart as these kids are, they had been lead to believe that the only way their parents could get them to behave was to treat them like prisoners. But once I challenged them to think critically about that, they realized that it really wasn't effective, that they didn't like it, and that they'd never stopped to think about any of it before.

That's how you, the parent, got to where you are. You accepted the way you were treated as a child. But we need to think critically about the ways we treat our kids, and basically, it comes down to this:

We need to treat our children as people. Doing otherwise is not good for children, parents, or society at large.

Some of the coolest and wisest people I've met have been children, and I never would have met them if I hadn't been ready to accept them as people and connect with them.

CORE PRINCIPLE 3:
PARENTING SHOCKER! IT'S NOT ABOUT YOU!

You can deny thinking it's all about you, but I wouldn't even have to mention the first two principles if we weren't coming from such a self-absorbed mindset. We are the smartest, we are the most informed. We know everything, and we are not to be disturbed from our pre-child lives—our children need to fit in with us. We. Are. The. Rulers. And our goal is to survive the raising of our kids with our butts firmly planted on the throne. So we resort to buying, bribing, placating, ignoring, objectifying, manipulating, punishing, and more, to keep ourselves on the proverbial throne, with our child subjects at our feet.

You focus on your job, because you want to be the best. You focus on earning more money, even when you have enough to cover the basics. You attempt to live vicariously—delusionally—through your children, because you didn't accomplish something you wanted to. You choose to rest on the weekends or hang out with your friends or the TV instead of being with your children. You put chores and endless to-do lists over your children. You attach the cell phone or the computer to your face, avoiding interaction with your children. You send your kids to their rooms because you want to unwind from "your long day," as though your kids spent the day at the spa.

Movie score of violins to raise your emotional empathy

Many parents admit to me that they thought a baby would magically repair the distress of their lives. It didn't.

Having a baby, like finding a mate, does not magically cure what ails us.

And when parents discover this, they often revert back to a pre-child mentality and *endure* the child they've brought into the world.

When this happens, the parents know they aren't putting in 100%, and they feel guilty about putting themselves first and turning a blind eye to their less-than-stellar treatment of their kids. The parents' self-esteem goes in the toilet, further fracturing themselves and their children.

And while I maintain that this parenting business is not ALL about you, it IS about you to some degree, because if you don't feel confident in your parenting, then you're headed in a downward spiral, and it's not going to end well for anyone.

You'll just keep enduring, trudging through this burden of parenthood. And like a Midwestern spring, it's over in a flash. Your children are 18, and you never really engaged with them. You missed their childhood, because you were too involved in your own life.

The vast majority of parents, even those who author parenting blogs, sigh and go for the hope of not doing *too* much damage to their children. I'm here to tell you that you can get that half-hearted every-parent mentality out of your brain. It is possible to raise whole, healthy, independent kids. But you can't do it if your heart isn't in it. So commit yourself to making the effort for your kids. They're worth it, and so are you.

Trying Won't Make You Successful at Your 24 Hour Job

In dance class, I often hear students say, "Yes. I'll try." Whenever this happens, my older students smile, because they know my "I'll try" demo is coming.

I lay a piece of paper on the floor and say to my student, "Go ahead. Try to pick up that paper." The student leans forward, and just as his fingers get close to the paper, I stop him. "Uh-uh. *Try* to pick it up." Now, some students get my point right away; others reach for the paper again, and I say, "Nope. You can't pick up. I want to see what *trying* to pick it up looks like for you." Then we both smile.

You can't "try" anything. You either do it successfully, or, if you are unsuccessful, you learn from your feedback and set about practicing or getting more coaching. The techniques in this book are no different. You have to practice, and you have to show some effort.

Half-hearted attempts to implement the Hanson Method, with a back up plan of going back to sit on your throne, are not going to get you the results you're looking for.

That kind of approach is all about you, and not about that little innocent face that follows you around the house—and will soon enough be out the door. Don't let that happen. Do your job.

Your job is to raise whole and independent children who can function as adults, without a host of emotional issues. This means that your child needs to come first. Many parents do not realize how important their own actions are to the achievement of this goal.

Your child will not be whole, and will not reach her fullest potential, without your love and fitting guidance. I have learned over the years to love children best by treating them as people and appropriately pushing them towards their independence, especially independence from self-limiting beliefs and actions from what I call DUBOOs – Dried Up Bits of Ourselves™ (think of them as crappy internal boo-boos.)

Negative interactions and experiences, served up from their parents in particular, are the toxins that dry up bits of our children's wholeness thereby creating hollow spaces inside where the whole part existed.

Now, left with emptiness and Dried Up Bits of Ourselves – DUBOOs –inside, we are not only unable to engage in life with a joyful, curious and engaged-in-the-moment style that is part of our true self, but we actually become "taken over" with the DUBOO's need to act up and act out because for many of us, we become controlled by them.

We lose our right mind from time to time.

Every time children are yelled at, dragged along, not taken care of, manipulated, threatened, punished, left, or otherwise harmed, the "blows" from their parent shrink parts of themselves –creating DUBOOs. Every time. Children may not show it in that moment, but they have absorbed it and it will come out later as inappropriate behavior. As an adult, they might be able to work around some of the damage they internalized from your actions, but it will make their life much more tedious and sad; some people never recover from the damage done to them, living their whole lives in a cycle of denial and pain.

Not too many parents want to intentionally damage their children nor have their children back on their doorsteps after college and/or indefinitely.

Hollowed children cannot be independent and pain-free adults, because they will always be looking to resuscitate the DUBOOs to restore their wholeness.

Unfortunately the poisonous beliefs residing inside the DUBOOs seek like energy. Negative attracts negative energy. The DUBOOs will seek out experiences and people to further wound them unless the person does something about it. They will limit themselves by seeking out unhealthy mates, situations, and friends; forming self-limiting habits (such as procrastination, lack of follow through, excessive worrying, pouting, manipulating, avoiding, frequent rage, depression, negativity, or inability to plan, organize, or manage time); or developing addictions (to alcohol, drugs, shopping, gambling, overeating, perilous risk taking, need to control, etc.). The Dried Up Bits of Ourselves, DUBOOs, dominate lives, and adult children will be dependent on bad situations to try to "heal themselves," rather than being independent, free to experience and explore life and pursue their passions.

Children are born whole, and they need to remain whole in order to become independent, and to reach their fullest potential.

It is up to you, the parents, to love your children, to leave their whole spirits INTACT, *and to push them toward independence.* Your children will love you for it.

I'm not implying that every minute has to be dedicated to your child. I understand that you need time to work, do chores, exercise, and have a date night. However many of these things can be done in concert with your child, in addition to each of you having time alone. With my methods and core principles in place, you will have the serenity and inspiration to be creative and discover unique activities to do together. Maybe you can designate a two-hour period for each family member to spend as he or she desires, followed by a family activity. Once you have some strategies at your disposal and are living in the moment, your confidence will increase.

At the end of the day, you can either leave your child's inborn perfection intact, or you can destroy it. But it's never too late to heal the traumas distancing you and your child from each other. With just a little bit of tweaking, you can connect with your child, be an outstanding parent, and avoid future wars.

The following story is an example of what can happen when you apply the Hanson Method and encourage a child to push past any previously acquired self-limiting fears.

Mission Control…We Have Lift Off

Leslie had just moved up to a higher-level acrobatics class, and acrobatics is a class where I always have to push children past their self-limiting beliefs. On this particular day, I was teaching a trick in which students run down the mat and launch themselves in the air over another student in a straddle headstand. Basically, the running student had to run, jump, fly through the air, clear the student in the headstand, and finish in a fast forward roll. In preparation, I had everyone do this trick initially over a low object, and then built the objects up until they were as high as a person in a headstand. Although she was new to this class, Leslie was actually the highest jumper in her execution of the trick. I knew that would be a surprise to her, as well as her classmates.

When I told Leslie she would be performing the trick, she looked at me as though I had told her a large grizzly bear was standing behind her. In the old days, I would have gotten nervous for her. But now, I simply smiled and acknowledged the obvious: "Are you getting nervous?"

"Yes!" she exclaimed.

I said, "Well you have some choices. You can psyche yourself out and tell yourself in your head that you can't do it. Or I could yell and intimidate you to do it. Or you can do positive talk inside your

head and tell yourself you can do it—especially if I think you can."
(Of course I don't believe in yelling—I just threw that in for comic
relief in the face of her building concern.)

She chose the positive talk. Off she went, with a determined
look on her face. And she made it! Then I added another girl to the
headstand—now there were two, tucked together. Leslie went back
to looking like she was being stalked by a grizzly. I reminded her of
her choices, and again, she went with the positive talk.

Off she went running, and she flew even higher. Fantastic! We
all cheered and celebrated her. I told her that she would have this
valuable lesson inside of her forever. Whenever she was faced with a
challenge that she knew she could *probably* do, but was afraid of
being the first to try it, she just had to remember to talk positively to
herself. She could trust herself.

This process of positive self-talk and adult encouragement—
avoiding the self-doubt that plagues adults—leaves the child whole,
able to meet challenges and achieve success. It is a repeatable skill.
The next week, I added a third girl to the headstand grouping, and
Leslie flew right over them yet again. She was so proud of herself
that she told her whole family, including her grandparents.

Removing self-doubt—or avoiding its introduction into a
child's life in the first place—does not always mean pushing a child.
Sometimes it means recognizing that child's current limits and
working within them, as in the following story. Whereas Leslie had
been apprehensive and needed a push, Matilda, in my next story,
was dealing with real fear.

Houston…Lift Off is Scrubbed

In my three-year-old class, I have an activity where the students run
across the room into their parents' arms for a ballet lift. It's always a fun
departure from the usual class, and the children love it. On this particular day, they were barely able to contain themselves, they were so
excited. Except for one little girl named Matilda. She had her face

buried, with both of her hands on her mouth, fidgeting. In the old days, I would have given a cheerleader's "Come on Matilda, you can do it!" but I know better now. The cheerleader does little with the younger set.

I went over, squatted down, and quietly said, "Hi Matilda. What's going on?" (Notice I didn't say, "Why are you afraid?")

She looked at me. No answer.

So I went with the obvious: "Do you not want to be lifted up high?"

"Yes."

I said, "So you have gone up high before and didn't like it?"

"Yes."

"Ok, I'll tell dad," I replied. "Dad," I said, "Matilda is going to run down to you, but she doesn't want to be lifted up."

Dad said, "Sure!"

And off Matilda went in her little bourrée run.

I didn't know her dad, but I can tell you that many a parent would have been embarrassed that his child wasn't doing something like the others and would have made a big scene, arguing, pleading, or grabbing the child and going home. Matilda's dad didn't do that, and so she had the opportunity to build her three-year-old confidence to do the lift in the future, once she can trust that she is safe. Remember, trust in others is built through consistently being treated well.

It is important to recognize a child's real fears, without projecting our own adult fears onto them.

Many times parents discourage their children from doing things that able-bodied children can do: sledding, bike riding, acrobatics class, dancing in pointe shoes, jumping on a trampoline, taking 2 or 3 dance classes in one day, diving, driving at 16, or attending that first teenage party, to name a few. I understand that when you have raised your children from an infant and you remember the helpless phases, it's easy to want to continue to do for them 24/7, but that only works up until they start to walk. Then it's time to start encouraging them—to walk, to run, to dance, to lift off! You might think they'll fall or be nervous or exhausted. And they might. But that is part of growing up into a strong, independent person.

The great thing about dance teachers is that we are fearless, always pushing. We don't care about the parents' fears. We care about the children's dreams. And we encourage them to go for it.

INDEPENDENCE VS. WILLFULNESS

There's a difference between "independent" and "willful." Independence is functioning well alone. Willful children don't know how to function, because their parents haven't taught them how. These parents treat their children like wild animals, allowing them to do whatever they want. When parents teach their children the decorum of a classroom, or a restaurant, or a store, the children are much happier, and so are the parents.

In life, most of us only do what we have to do, and if we can get away with the bare minimum, we'll go for that. It's human nature. I'm here to tell you that being a great parent does not take monumental effort on your part. All it takes is a shift in mindset.

Ditch the idea of parenting as you know it, treat your child like a human being, and encourage him to grow into a healthy, independent adult.

You will be amazed at the results.

THE SIX STEPS TO SANITY™

Now that you know the three Core Principles of the Hanson Parenting Method, I will share with you my number one technique that has proven 100% effective over the years for dealing with any kind of conflict you have with your child. In fact, the Six Steps to Sanity work for any kind of conflict you have with *anyone*—including your spouse.

> *The Six Steps to Sanity set the stage for a beautiful relationship between you and your child, rooted in healthy communication, mutual respect, and unconditional love.*

Used consistently, this tool will have you well on your way to raising a whole and independent child, capable of the highest level of performance in dance and in life.

STEP #1: SLOW – WAY – DOWN – AND – BREATHE

You need to remove yourself from the fast pace of life in order to be in the moment and ready to really communicate with your child.

> *Aim for slowing down so much that you're almost in slow motion.*

Can you remember an experience in your life where you felt like you were in slow motion? Think of waking up—maybe not in the morning, because some mornings we jump out of bed in a hurry to make an appointment. The slow motion I'm going for is more like waking up from a long, languorous vacation nap, or coming out of sedation after surgery. If you can get yourself into that state where you are not thinking of anything else, you will be without emotion and in a state of simple *being*—a.k.a. love—and ready for the adventure of discovering something new about your child. You're in slow motion, but you're awake, and you're prepared to handle whatever comes your way.

Now, breathe. Have you ever noticed how our breathing becomes shallow when we are nervous? You have to counteract that effect. Many people say to breathe from your belly, but that's not enough. I want you *breathe with your whole body*, and on the inhale, run the breath from your toes all the way to the top of your head. Breathe with the body's molecules. Do it right now. Do you see how shallow your breath was before? Two to three will do wonders to oxygenate your body, allowing its systems to calm down.

Throughout this discussion with your child, if you don't know what to say, simply slow down and breathe deeply. Creative insight will come to you if you remain calm and open.

STEP #2: STOP THE FLOOD OF OLD PATTERNS AND JUDGMENT. GET CURIOUS

When we panic, we instantly access our brains, going back through time to remember how we handled a similar situation. If we don't have any first-hand parenting experience with a particular situation, we end up back at how our parents did it. Or if we somehow avoid parenting the way our parents did, we jump to conclusions based on an amalgamation of societal beliefs. And if we're relying on these old patterns, we aren't thinking. We are reacting.

You need to get curious in order to respond to the moment in front of you.

Banish the assumptions. You can't be curious if you think you already know what's going on.

Imagine you've just come out of the grocery store. Your child gets in the car and opens a pack of batteries for his handheld videogame—a pack of batteries you know you didn't pay for. What do you do?

The common reaction is to go into panic mode. In thousandths of a second, you are sifting through your own past to see if there is any protocol for "child stealing batteries." If not, your brain switches to asking, "What would society at large do?" Suddenly, judgmental words like "thief" "criminal" "lifer in prison" and "death penalty" are flooding your brain, and the impulse to save your child before the police get to him is dictating your actions. A variety of typical parenting moves might ensue: a) marching him into the store and humiliating him via the store manager's reprimand; b) congratulating your child on a job well done; c) beating the crap out of him and destroying his videogame; d) grounding him for a month; e) yelling "Why in the hell did you do that? Are you a thief now?" or f) just driving off, because you're confused about what you should do. All of these actions are ineffective, because they don't get to the root of why your child took the batteries in the first place—or why he shouldn't do it again.

Instead, stop the panic before it starts. Slow way down and breathe deeply.

Clear your mind of assumptions, and get curious about the situation.

Remember that your child is a person, and there are many possible reasons why he may have taken the batteries. Maybe a friend told him it was okay. Maybe he saw a sign that said, "Get one free," and so he did. Maybe he didn't know that when you were all the way up there swiping your card through that machine with the buttons, you were actually paying for things, and that that's required when you take things from a store. (Have you explained credit cards? Can you?) Whatever the reason was, you'll never know if you panic and let the old patterns and assumptions take over. So get curious.

When you get curious, your child can sense the lightness and openness in your manner, and she will be more relaxed, almost playful. This is the perfect mood for a highly intelligent and profound conversation with you—even at age 2. When you are calm and curious, you and your child are ready for the next step.

STEP #3: GREET YOUR CHILD AT EYE-LEVEL, IN A SOFT VOICE

I'm talking about a real greeting here—something along the lines of "Hello, will you join me," or "May we talk and share?" Smile. Say, "Thank you for joining me." Your kids know the difference between a genuine invitation and "Come over here and see if I'm going to take your head off." Pretend you're inviting a nun over to join you for high tea, if that helps.

It is important not to tower over your child. That's intimidating even between adults, but especially for a small child. *Aim for eye-to-eye level.* If you are 6' 5" and your child is three, put her on a chair while you sit on the floor. Or you can both sit on the floor, even if you aren't exactly eye to eye—it takes you back to when you were a child, and that helps bring you to your child's level metaphorically as well. Also, *respect your child's space* and maintain the socially accepted standard of 3 feet between you.

Throughout this discussion with your child, *maintain a soft voice.* This is quite important, and it applies to fathers, as well. Using a gentle voice sends your child the message that you aren't interested in hurting him. It helps you remain calm and curious. When I say soft and gentle, by the way, I do not mean tearful and whimpering. Lower your voice, but be confident.

STEP #4: INQUIRE CANDIDLY AND RESPECTFULLY, AND REALLY LISTEN TO THE ANSWER

Your goal here is to get right to the issue within 2-3 sentences; otherwise you're pursuing your own agenda. Be respectful of your child's time, and don't waste yours. *Stick to the point, and ASK your child what's going on.* "Why" questions often put people on the defensive, but if you ask it the right way—gently, and out of real curiosity, kids will generally answer.

Sometimes you might need to recap your observation of events so that your child knows what you're talking about. That's okay, but be straightforward and succinct. You don't need to walk on egg-shells. Just tell the truth. Many adults have a fear of conflict, but that's your own mess to deal with.

> *You need to understand what's going on in your child's head, so that you can respectfully teach her the things she needs to know to become a whole and independent person.*

Being respectful to them does not mean being timid, holding back. Be direct. Don't get angry and hope she can figure it all out based upon your upset face. Just get to the point.

Next, when your child answers your question, stay calm, curious, and available to hear him. *Really listen to your child's answer.* It's common for children to automatically respond with an "I don't know," so if that happens, that means he needs some reassurance. You can say something like, "'I don't know' just means that you're uncomfortable about telling me, but I am really curious and you can tell me the truth." The next sentence out of his mouth will be a real answer. Adults have learned to layer their answers many times over, but children get right to it. They love to be direct, if you encourage them. But whatever you do, do not *attack* your child when he tells you the truth, or he will never open up again. Build confidence. Build his trust.

STEP #5: DISCUSS THE SITUATION WITH LOVE, AND DECIDE ON A COURSE OF ACTION TOGETHER

Now that you and your child both understand what the problem is, you need to come to a decision about how to address it. With a young child, the course of action will be a no-brainer: you really aren't going to let her play in zero-degree weather without a coat, for example. *But it's important to develop the skill set of working together,* so that when tougher issues come up in the future, you have that breadcrumb trail to follow through the forest of "Argh!

What do I do here?!"

Remember: stay calm. If you need to, use those deep breaths again. Emotion on either end of the spectrum—from hostility to worthlessness—precludes the state of love.

Leave your emotions out of it.

If you let your emotions interfere in this discussion with your child, you will bring your own agenda and your own fractured bits of yourself into the discussion, and that will only attract negativity. This discussion should not be about your fear of your child or her reactions, and it should not involve manipulation. It should be about lovingly upholding your basic rules to promote your child's wholeness and independence.

STEP #6: FOLLOW UP

Children love it when adults are dependable. They love dealing with adults who keep their word. At the end of this Six Step dialog, you have a golden opportunity to convey your genuine interest in your child and whatever discovery you both have gotten to. Tell your child you want to follow up to see how this new revelation is working out—and then follow through on your word. Depending on the situation, it might be appropriate to follow up after an hour or a week. Or, depending on the nature of the issue, you may not need a follow up, because the issue is completely resolved. Following up is another demonstration of your investment in your child's world—without which, they cannot become amazing.

The art of keeping your word is waning in today's world. We have too many "acceptable" excuses. Go out of your way to be dependable and follow up, and your child will come to know that you are a parenting rock star.

Olga: Over and Out

One afternoon, I got a knock on my office door, and when I answered it, there was five-year-old Olga, with her mom behind her. I had done some parent coaching with Olga's mom, and she was letting Olga handle things herself here, which was great.

Olga looked up at me with the biggest puppy eyes fringed with long lashes, and said, "I don't want to take dance class anymore."

What a great time to use the Six Steps to Sanity! Immediately, I deployed:

Step #1: Slow – way – down – and – breathe.

I was not expecting to have to deal with this problem, but life doesn't give you engraved invitations to upcoming challenges, so I consciously slowed myself down. I breathed deeply as I took in Olga's surprising statement. Next, I moved right on to:

Step #2: Stop the flood of old patterns and judgments and get curious.

Really, I didn't know what was motivating Olga's decision, and I was very curious to know.

Calm and curious, I was ready for:

Step #3: Greet the child at eye-level, in a soft voice.

Since Olga had initiated the conversation, I didn't have to greet her, but I did invite her to sit with me.

Now that we were at eye-level with each other, we were ready for:

Step #4: Inquire candidly and respectfully, and really listen to the answer.

I responded to her initial statement, saying, "I wasn't expecting to hear that today, Olga. So tell me why you have come to this decision to not take dance class?"

Olga responded triumphantly, "I want to be home with mommy." I was thrilled, because a) she had told me the real reason behind her decision, and b) the work I had done with her mom had transformed her so much that Olga, who LOVED dance, wanted to be with her *new* mommy.

Now it was time for:

Step #5: Discuss the situation with love, and decide on a course of action together.

Careful to keep my emotions out of the discussion, I replied, "I don't blame you. She IS a cool mom." We sat in silence for a few seconds.

Olga continued, "She's fun now."

I said, "I bet. So let's figure all this out. You are enrolled in a dance class, right?"

Olga said, "Yes."

I said, "And you want to be with mom, right?"

"Yes," said Olga.

I said, "What will you do when she has to be at work and can't be here during your lesson?"

Olga squished her face up for a second and, looking at me with those puppy eyes, responded very seriously, "Well, she just won't work anymore."

A typical response to such a suggestion might be laughter, but laughing would have belittled Olga, and it would not have been respectful. Instead, I remained as though I were in a board meeting. "I see," I replied, "Now, what about when you are in school, and mom is at home? What should she do? She might miss you."

Olga thoughtfully answered, "Well she could play with my dolls until I got home."

Still serious, I said, "Ahh. That's an idea. Well, it's sort of like each of us has to do what we have to do in life. You have to go to school and mom has to go to work. Do you agree?"

Even though Olga didn't want her mom to work, she was very reasonable when it was put this way. She responded, "Yes."

I continued, "So we agree, then, that you each have something to do during the day?" Olga nodded.

I went on, "Then the real issue is that when you get off from school, some days mom has to be at work, and some days she can be with you right after school, right?"

Olga said, "Yeah. I just want her to pick me up from school every day."

I said, "I bet. That would be fun." Pause. "Oh, but wait. I forgot. You have something to do after school. You have dance class on a couple of days."

We both looked at each other like, "Oh, riiighht."

I said, "Well, you have some choices, then. You could drop dance class and sit at home and wait for mom to get home from what she has to do, which is work; or you could take dance class, which is kind of like your work. And then after class, she could pick you up. What do you think?"

I could see by the look on Olga's face that the gears were turning in her mind. Finally, she said, "I don't think so, because I would still miss her." Olga's five-year-old frontal lobe was having a little difficulty putting all the pieces together. She was close, but she wanted what she wanted.

I said, "Actually, you had a great idea earlier Olga." She perked up with hope. I said, "Remember when you said mom could play with your dolls while you were at school? Well, what if you both got a little trinket to have with each of you every day so you could know that she was thinking of you, and you could remember her? Maybe a special necklace called a locket, or a ribbon on your backpack and on her briefcase?"

Olga smiled and looked at her mom. Her mom said, "That sounds great. We can talk about what to get."

Ah, we had reached a solution. Now it was time for:

I said, "This sounds great, Olga. You get to go to school and dance and get smarter and smarter, and mom gets to go to work and then run to see you the second she is done. And you can both think of each other during the day. Does that sound cool?"

Olga's face was bright with joy, and she said, "Yes!"

I said, "Okay, we have a plan. Will you do me a favor, Olga? Will you please stop and find me and show me what it is you both decide on to be your special trinket?"

She agreed, and out she went with her mom. Two days later, Olga came running up to show me that they had both gotten little plastic animal-shaped bracelets. Mom was the height of office fashion with hers, and proud that she could do such a small thing to comfort her daughter.

When do you use the Six Steps? As soon after the problem event as possible. You don't want to avoid discussing problems as they come up, and then have to use the Six Steps to address a 10-issue pileup, where no one can keep track of what is being said. Address problems as they arise, stick to the point, and move on.

My experience with Olga is a wonderful story of how to use the Six Steps to Sanity with a young child to address a hot button problem for working moms and dance teachers everywhere. This is but one example among many, and you will see lots more as you read through the book.

If you're just getting used to the Hanson Method, the skills involved in the Six Steps to Sanity may feel like foreign territory to you. Let me assure you that children are highly invested in moving toward peace—more so than adults. Take a deep breath, write the steps down on a piece of paper if you need to, carry it with you into the conversation for reference, and give it a try. The more you use the Six Steps, the more second nature they will become. You can do this, for your child and for yourself.

FROM
AMAZING
KIDS

CHAPTER TWO

WHAT'S LOVE GOT TO DO WITH IT?

The Hanson Method does not work without love. You can commit the three Core Principles and the Six Steps to Sanity to memory, but without love, they will do you no good at all.

Love is not an act or a profession, though its expression can be. Love is not expectation or requirement. Love is not a gift in wrapping paper.

Love *is*. You have to *be* love. Infants naturally evoke your love just by being themselves; they are love, and it resonates in you. They don't have to say anything, do anything, bring you anything. Up until about age 6, children are uninhibited in their love and honesty. They will tell us if our breath smells bad, if we have acne, or if they don't think we're funny--and they are lavish with their love. Around age 7, they learn to hold back like everyone else— unless you engage them in love.

Children's innocence starts to fade and their wholeness starts to dehydrate, not because they get older, but because they are exposed to stress and non-love. Our stress, put onto our children, creates their dried-up bits of our children which seek unhealthy energy in a futile attempt to heal. When children see a parent rushed, frustrated, or stressed, they shut down, just like a computer—always at the worst time, and you don't see it coming. This is a symptom of an unhealthy parent-child dynamic, and…

> … *it is you, the parent, who needs to change—not because you're the oldest, but because you are the one doing the damage.*

You have been on the planet longer; you have picked up more stresses. *You* change, and your child will ride right along, as your positive energy attracts their positive energy.

> *The fastest way back to love is to spend time with your children.*

Watch them, study them, play with them. Observe them not as a parent, but in wonderment. Move from a stressed state to a playful state. Watch not from burden, but from innocence.

We've all felt that state. Maybe upon waking, before we start thinking of the tasks of the day. Maybe when we're looking at a sleeping child. In this state, we feel particularly accepted and understood. We are without fear.

Love has no strings attached. It has no judgment, no expectation, no need for control. It is just inside you, waiting to be recognized. When we are operating out of love, we are motivated to kindness. We *want* to engage in activities, cook meals, give gifts, make positive comments, interact fairly, etc.—because these things resonate with our children.

Parent out of love, and your child will know it. So how do you get there? First, remember the three Core Principles of the Hanson Method.

> *Wake up and be in the moment, treat your child as a person, and foster her wholeness and independence. That will create the love state in you.*

Of course, we all have to deal with the stress of the world, and sometimes it's hard to break away from that long enough to actually remember those three Core Principles, isn't it? Well, that's what the Six Steps to Sanity are for. The very first step—slow down and breathe deeply—is the easiest way I know to get you out of your head and into your heart. We can't be in a state of love 24/7, but we can aim to get there at least when we engage with our children.

WHAT LOVE IS NOT

"Parenting" has taken the idea of love and twisted it into many things it is not. Love is not bribery: "I'll buy this for you if you do your dance class without getting in trouble." Love is not approval: "Be how I want you to be so that I can like you." Love is not hitting: "This hurts me more than it hurts you." Love is not threats: "You'd better do great onstage, or that Xbox I bought you is going back to the store."

> *Such abuse of love is where the damage starts—and it's ineffective, to boot.*

Connive a child, and that child will connive you right back. Control a child's personality, and she will resent you. Buy his attention, and you will lose his respect.

Pink Slippers, Pink Tights, Pink Leotard…Pink Bike?

A few years ago, an eight-year-old dancer named Rhonda was at the studio with her mom, Pearl. I overheard Pearl say to Rhonda, "If you take ballet all the rest of this term and finish, I'll buy you the pink bike."

This was something that needed to be discussed, so, as I do in any discussion, I implemented my Six Steps. First, I slowed myself down and breathed deeply *(Step #1)*, and then I cleared my mind of any feelings I had about the possibility that Pearl hated ballet *(Step #2: Stop the flood of old patterns and judgment. Get curious)*. I invited them both into my office to sit down, and I greeted them at eye level, in a soft voice *(Step #3)*. When they were settled, I initiated *Step #4: Inquire candidly and respectfully, and really listen to the answer*. "I hear about an exciting pink bike offer. I am curious. Did I hear correctly that if Rhonda does ballet, she gets a bike?"

Pearl said, "We agreed that she would take ballet, and now she says it's boring. I think that if she just sticks with it, she'll end up liking it, so I just wanted to give her some incentive to hang in there."

I turned to Rhonda and asked her what was going on.

"Ballet is boring. I want to stop."

I can't get anywhere with the parent in the room, so I asked Pearl to step out to the hall so I could continue with *Step # 5: Discuss the situation with love, and decide on a course of action together*. I asked Rhonda, "Who wants you to do ballet more, you or your mom?"

She said, "First it was me, but now it's mom."

"Thanks for sharing that," I said. We sat a few seconds in silence. Then I asked, "Do you remember when it got boring?"

"Sort of. When I knew that we have to do the same thing every class, like pliés. We don't get to do the stuff in the older kids' class," she admitted.

"Well, thanks again for being so honest. That's great," I replied. Then I continued, "Do you know how those kids get to do all those cool things?"

She shook her head.

"They had to do what you do. They took the beginners' class, and then the next level and the one after that, and they still do pliés every class. They want to be really great dancers, and they know they have to work super hard and try to never miss a class." I paused and let that sink in. Then I asked, "Do you want to be a good dancer?" It was a valid question, allowing her to focus on her goals.

"Yes! I do," she said.

"Well, it's going to take a lot of work. More work than anything I can think of doing. Harder than learning to play a sport or a musical instrument. Harder than math. To be a great dancer, you have to work hard. Do you want to do that?"

"Yes!" Rhonda exclaimed.

"Well, that's great that you know what you want. See, when you know what you want, then you can work really hard."

She said she could. I went on, "Now the thing about the pink bike—you know that is bribery, right?"

She said, "Yeah, Mom likes to do that. But I want to do ballet, so she doesn't have to do that."

I asked, "Do you sometimes know that if you act like you don't want to do something, that she'll—"

Rhonda finished my sentence, "Buy me stuff. Yeah, I know."

I said, "Do you think you would feel good about yourself if you did the ballet just because of the bike?"

"Oh, no. I want to do it on my own. For me."

Now it was time for *Step #6: Follow Up*. "Rhonda," I said, "That sounds like an excellent plan. Come and see me after ballet next week and tell me if the class felt different when you were looking at it as a way to make yourself better, without getting a prize."

Remember, kids do not want their love bought off. It cheapens them and your relationship.

Real love can't be bought.

Love is. Act out of love. Your life will become remarkable.

ABOUT A

CHAPTER THREE

BE POSITIVE

Be positive on every level. Children soak up positivity; it's a lifeline to their potential. But somewhere along the line, parents have gotten some wrong ideas about how to parent. Maybe their parents did it; maybe they are frustrated with life, having been fractured as children. I'm here to tell you about the power of positivity. Being positive is your way of creating your own heaven for you and for your child.

BE POSITIVE BECAUSE IT WORKS

Catch your child doing something right and be positive about it. Watch how that blossoms to other things. I have some tween students who will adopt a defeatist attitude if I give them one correction at the beginning of the class. However, if I say one positive comment instead, they are on fire the whole class.

When was the last time that someone railed at you over and over and you decided, "Gee, now I agree with them."? Probably never.

Children are no different, and that is why nagging doesn't work.

Let's differentiate between nagging and educating. According to TheFreeDictionary.com, "nagging" is defined as:

1   To annoy by constant scolding, complaining, or urging.
2   To torment persistently, as with anxiety or pain.
3   To scold, complain, or find fault constantly.

Here is my favorite definition, though: "Nag" is the name of a certain type of tank destroyer missile known as "fire and forget." How perfect. The parent fires off a directive, and the kid forgets it.

I believe that children only need to hear something once or twice. If you need to repeat yourself more often than that, you're doing something wrong.

For example, if a child repeatedly forgets to put his hat on in the winter, many parents would say something like, "Jonathon, I swear you'd leave your brain behind if it wasn't attached. For the fiftieth time, put your hat on!" Here's the deal. Either Jonathon is warm enough without the hat, or it bothers him in some way. (Maybe it's scratchy, or it doesn't fit well.) And nagging isn't going to make one bit of difference.

To avoid the pitfall of nagging, you must educate instead. This means telling your child to do something not because you said so, but because there is value in it. You should explain *why* your child should do something that impacts her health, safety, or well being. However that value shouldn't include your personal preferences, as your child may have different preferences. If you can't find real value in something, then you don't need to ask your child to do it in the first place.

In the case of Jonathon and his hat, the first thing to do would be to find out *why* he doesn't want to wear his hat, and then work from there. If he's warm enough without it, maybe he really doesn't need to wear it. If he's warm now, but you know that you'll be out for a while, and he'll probably get cold later, explain that to him.

Maybe he could put it in his pocket for later. If there's something wrong with the hat, see if you can address the problem in some way.

Educating your child requires that you view him as a person, and communicate with him.

Some dance parents ask, "But shouldn't I let my child know she needs to work harder to point her foot (or straighten her back or lift her leg higher)?" No. Let her teacher tell her. A smart dancer is having that dialogue with herself anyway. Three's a crowd. If she asks you, say "I always love it when I see you with that fantastic straight back of yours." What you can say before she goes into class is, "Cooperate with your teacher and focus to get the most out of class." You can say this even if she is two.

BE POSITIVE WITH YOUR WORDS

About the time my grandson was 2½ -3, whenever he did something creative, thoughtful, smart, helpful, etc., I commented about how it had value, and then I would say, "I like that about you." This is huge for a child.

Tell your child what you like about him—what makes him unique.

Don't use words to label your child—it's demoralizing. Your little one is looking to you, one of the people she loves the most, and being herself. And what does she get? A label. Not only does this dry up a little bit of her real self, but labels are self-perpetuating.

For example, sometimes, when a young child does not want to say "Hello" when introduced to an adult, her parent will say something like, "Julie is shy," often in a most dramatic fashion.

I've never met a shy child. I've met young children who are appropriately leery of a towering new adult face. Why should they have to eek out a "Hello" when they barely speak? So that the parents will look like they did a good job parenting? Tell her she's shy, and guess what? She will be. That's no way to encourage her to be independent.

Instead of labeling your child as shy, validate her instinct to be wary around new adults. You could say something to her like, "Yeah, you don't know him yet, do you?" Introduce her to others, but skip the pressure to conform in a way that will make you look good as a parent. It's not like she'll never learn to say "Hello." When she's older and more confident of her ability to size someone up, she'll be fine.

It's also popular among parents to tell their two-year-olds to share their toys. Most two-year-olds, however, are not developmentally ready for sharing. They don't really play with other kids; they play next to them. A two-year-old can't see the value in sharing. So what happens when he balks at being asked to share his toys? Often, the parent will say something like, "He's not much of a sharer. He's selfish." Not only is this incorrect—a two-year-old refusing to share his toys is not selfish; he's *normal*—but it's also detrimental, because labels have a way of sticking.

Instead of asking your child to do something he's not developmentally ready to do, you could re-direct him (or the child with whom he's not sharing) to a different toy or activity. Later, when he's old enough to appreciate the value in sharing, you can help him learn about that skill. And in the meantime, if you need to say something about the situation at all (for example, if the other child he's playing with is older and deserves some kind of explanation), you could say something positive, like "Joey's still learning how to share."

BE POSITIVE IN RESPONSE TO YOUR CHILD'S AILMENTS

Do not indulge your dance child's every ache and pain. If your child tells you something hurts, you can say, "Oh, I understand. I get aches and pains, too. Do you think you can carry on, or do we need to take you to the hospital?" This exaggeration tends to lighten the mood. In life we all have to carry on with a headache, sniffles, etc. (I'm assuming you would know when there is something majorly wrong.)

I have a dance mother who writes a note every week to excuse her daughter from class for this or that. Every week.

I'm all for believing children, but if a child has an ailment of the week every week, there is something else going on.

Ask the dance studio if they have any observation of a possible issue.

Stretching Makes It Better

One time, a five-year-old named Susan went missing from class for three weeks. We called her mother, who said that her daughter had suddenly decided she didn't want to come to dance, so they quit. I asked the mother to bring Susan into the studio to talk to me. She did. When they arrived, I asked the mother to sit in the hallway, while Susan came into my office to talk. I offered Susan a chair. I slowed down and took my deep breaths *(Step #1)*; I cleared my head of possible reasons she didn't want to attend class anymore and focused on just Susan *(Step #2)*.

"Hi Susan. Thanks for coming to talk to me," I greeted her. *(Step #3)* "I've missed you in dance class."

"I know, it just hurted so much," said Susan.

"Oh," I replied. "What part of class caused a hurt?" *(Step #4: Inquire candidly and respectfully, and really listen to the answer)*.

"The stretching," she said.

"Yes, it does feel like it hurts. But really it's the muscles saying, 'Okay, I'm getting stretched out to be a good dancer.' If you keep doing it, that feeling goes away."

"Ok, I'll come back to dance," Susan proudly announced. (Although it was a short discussion, because we resolved the issue quickly, this was *Step #5: Discuss the situation with love, and decide on a course of action together.*)

"Great, Susan!" I said, "I want to follow up with you in the next few classes to see if stretching starts to feel better," (*Step #6: Follow Up*).

By remaining positive in the face of Susan's physical complaints (and using my Six Steps to Sanity to communicate with her about them), I avoided a dance student casualty.

BE POSITIVE IN RESPONSE TO YOUR CHILD'S EMOTIONS

Sometimes children come out of dance and say, "I hate dance." Many parents respond, "Oh, okay. We won't go back." This astounds me. Have you never expressed a fleeting feeling, which went away an hour later? Do you quit over such a feeling? I hope not.

It is important for you to hear your child's emotions. And then…don't do anything. Just be there to hear. Sometimes that is all that we need. Parents seem compelled to do away with their child's negative emotions. If your child said, "I love my puppy," would you go buy another puppy?

We don't need to double their positive or eradicate their negative emotions.

Just let them be expressed so that they don't lead to something else.

A Sour Note

A teacher came to my office from her classroom with a five-year-old boy who was being unusually difficult.

He shouted, "I'm not strong for dance."

The teacher left, and I invited the boy to sit with me. I slowed myself down and breathed deeply *(Step #1)*, shifting my focus away from paying bills. I have been doing the Six Steps for a long time, so I've gotten pretty good at avoiding snap judgments. But a typical thought that someone might have to banish at this point might be

"Oh, here's another bad mood I have to deal with, and I'm busy. Why me?!" I avoided such thoughts, and just focused on Carlos (*Step #2*), saying, "Hey, Carlos. What's going on?" (*Step #3: Greet at eye-level, in a soft voice*).

Scowling, he said, "Nuthin'. I'm not a good dancer."

"That's interesting," I said. I knew he loved dance, so I wasn't going to lay on the typical syrupy "you're so good" stuff. He didn't need his ego stroked. Something was clearly wrong. I went to the start of the day and asked, "Did everything go okay at home before school today?" (*Step #4: Inquire candidly and respectfully, and really listen to the answer*).

"Yeah." Pause. Then he burst out, "I had to play the violin at school today in front of everyone, and I made a mistake." He looked up at me as if to see if I still liked him.

I said, "Wow. If that happened to me I might feel embarrassed. Did you?"

Carlos nodded, a tear falling.

I went on, "I have danced onstage in front of people and messed up. But then I found out a big secret."

He looked at me.

I continued, "Nobody else knew I'd made a mistake. Just me. Then, when I got older, I realized that *everyone* makes mistakes," (*Step #5: Discuss the situation with love, and decide on a course of action together*).

He looked so relieved. (At that point his dad popped in, saw that I had it covered, and left. Very cool on the dad's part, letting his son figure things out on his own at age 5.)

The storm on Carlos' face had passed. He felt okay again.

I said, "Would you like me to walk you back to class?"

"Yes."

"Carlos," I said, "Let me know if you ever feel like you need to talk, will you?" I knew that the issue of the moment was resolved, but I wanted to leave the door open for more conversations in the future (*Step #6: Follow Up*).

Sometimes, your child might come to you frustrated about not being able to get a particular dance step. Encourage this dialogue so she can vent, but remain neutral. Tell your child simply that you trust that with her talent and dedication, she will get it. If the frustration continues over time, you can always ask the studio if private lessons are in order. Let your child learn how to process her emotions. That is a step towards independence and dealing with her whole self—even the frustrating parts.

BE POSITIVE ABOUT YOUR CHILD'S PEERS

If you are dissing other dancers or teammates in an effort to boost your child's esteem, you are losing twice. Those classmates are your child's friends, or at the very least, peers. If your child hears you talking poorly about others, it will taint his outlook on his classmates, which can cause problems.

Even worse, if your dancer hears you judging other children, he will start to judge himself. He can't help but think that is the appropriate course of action to take with others and himself. And when a dancer starts judging himself, it's a downward spiral. The following story is an example of what can happen when a child is exposed to her parent's judgmentalism.

What Did You Say?!

Callie's mom was one of those witty moms who people gathered around—and that was part of the reason her criticism affected Callie so deeply. Seeing all those adults hanging on her mom's words, Callie figured her opinion carried weight. One afternoon, my office door was ajar, and Callie and her mother were outside in the hall. I overheard Callie's mother delivering her opinion of Callie's classmates.

"Trudy thinks she is good, but have you seen how big her butt is? She won't be a ballerina. You can't have that sticking out. Plus, she's mixed, and you have to be white. And that Vanessa is always off tempo in tap. She ruins the whole routine. I'd take her to the doctor to get her ears cleaned out, so she can hear."

Upon hearing this, I was a) mortified; and b) suddenly clued in to why Callie holds back in class—she's afraid of being judged by her own mother.

It's very easy for a child to think that as her mother judges, so does everyone else.

Callie is very hard on herself in class and looks wounded when she receives a correction on her technique. A dance student who is defensive in the face of a dance teacher's tips will make slow progress. A student who feels good about corrections can make adjustments and move on quickly to new dance challenges. Callie's mother should focus on Callie—positively—instead of on Callie's peers, in order to improve her own daughter's performance in dance.

And just for the record, ballerinas come in all ethnicities, heights, and shapes.

Clearly, criticizing your child's peers is not a good idea. In fact…

…don't comment on things AT ALL in your child's dance world

Dance is your child's passion, his connection to his soul. Allowing yourself to comment on small things, like "I don't like that part of the choreography" or "I don't like that costume" or "I don't like your place in the dance" only confuses your child, and it eventually leads you to bigger negatives, such as "Why aren't you in that higher level class?" "Why aren't you dancing the lead?" or "Why doesn't your teacher make you a better dancer?" You *are* entitled to your opinion, but you are *not* entitled to sharing it with your child. It is an immature impulse to give commentary when it is neither solicited nor necessary.

Your child does not need to struggle with fulfilling his passion *and* having to reconcile his love for dance (or any other passion, for that matter) with your apparent disdain for dance. He wants to love dance *and* you; he becomes split attempting to achieve two different goals. He is a child—even if he is 16. You want him to be amazing, so don't let your opinions stand in his way. He is not a miracle worker.

BE POSITIVE WITH YOUR CHILD'S DREAMS

One of my students told me that she was sitting at a Disney on Ice show, when she overheard the four-year-old boy next to her say to his mom, "There's Mickey!" His mother retorted, "No, that's an actor playing Mickey." Really? Did she have to go there?

As another of my students said, "If I am dreaming of being a ballerina, let me have that one. Don't tell me it doesn't pay well, and I'd better have a backup plan at college."

Let them have their dreams.

Who is a parent to tell a child what she needs to do? Are you a former employee of the Psychic Hotline?

And speaking of college, if parents' default Gotta-Teach-'em Top 10 starts with not being shy, it ends with, "You must finish college." Can you imagine if Bill Gates, Mark Zuckerberg, or Steve Jobs had been forced by their parents to finish college? Can you imagine Mark Zuckerberg's parents telling him to dream something other than Facebook? Or Bill Clinton's parents telling him to forget being president, because it was too much of a long shot? You have to let each child explore what comes up for her, not force your ideas onto her spirit.

Conversely, can you imagine that Michael Jordan or Tiger Woods would have made it big in their respective sports without their parents' attention? Magnus Carlsen, the number one chess player in the world at age 21, has always had his parent's support—in fact, the whole family took a year off to explore his love for chess when he was a child. Many parents don't even give their child an entire weekend of attention.

BE POSITIVE IN THE FACE OF YOUR CHILD'S EARNESTNESS

Please, don't mock your child. If your son says something technically incorrect, but he's using his toddler smarts, don't laugh at him. If your daughter falls down, don't make a joke out of it. This all comes under treating your child as a person.

No Laughing Matter

Every time we have in-class observation, I dread the mocking of an innocent child. At one such observation, when all the parents had gathered for the four-year-old ballet and tap class, I announced to the children that they were going to have so much fun at the upcoming recital.

One little girl, Puja, asked seriously, "*Why* will we have fun?"

The parents burst out laughing over the precocious question, but Puja had asked an excellent question that I valued. I had not educated the children enough about the recital to offer up any possible value, so why should she expect to have fun just because I said so? Good for Puja.

During that same class, Jessie's tap shoe flew off during a shuffle, and she slipped and fell. The parents laughed as though they were watching a comedian do a pratfall.

It's okay to laugh at a comedian, but not at a child who is trying her best.

I guarantee you if an adult did the same thing, nobody would have laughed—especially if the adult was upset.

If we keep the Core Principles in place, remembering that a whole, independent person is residing inside each child, and we engage in the most positive behavior possible, our children will blossom to greatness. Negative talk is like eating sugar—it's addictive, and it's bad for your health.

CHAPTER FOUR

MAKE AND ENFORCE RULES
(DON'T WASTE YOUR PRECIOUS TIME)

Over the years, I've had parents enroll their children not for dance, but for me to turn them into model citizens. It would be much better in the short term and the long term if the parents were facilitating that process.

When I walk into a classroom of three-year-olds on the first day of class, I spend five minutes telling them the rules of the classroom. I repeat this at the next class. The following three class meetings, I have them tell me the rules of the classroom. They always get them right. Then for the entire year I rarely have to ask them to comply.

The only three-year-olds who consistently break classroom rules are always the children of parents who don't enforce rules for them at home. These parents waste time every day hoping that their children will not do this or that. Or if they do tell their children the rules, they don't require them to cooperate. And sure enough, they don't.

If you want your child to start out correctly in dance or any group activity at any age, you need to make sure that you enforce your rules at home. Dance done well has many rules. It's not a Woodstock-ish "hey whatever feels good" environment. Children need to learn protocol, basics, and cooperation with the teacher, for starters. At the studio I enforce all of this, but if new children are conditioned to lawlessness at home, they spend most of my class trying to decide if they should follow my style or yours.

Now, why don't parents have rules or enforce them at home? Over the years I have discovered it is for one reason alone: they need their children to like them, because they don't like themselves.

Being a child's friend or being liked by a child should never be a parent's (or a teacher's) goal. Let their friends be their friends. You be the leader. They already love you.

> *Your children will not only like you if you are a consistently great leader, they will respect you.*

Every time you choose not to enforce a rule and let children run you over, you get chaos, and you lose time that could be spent better.

Does your child show up to dance class confused? Does your child laugh at the teacher when she asks him to stand in line, just like he laughs at you at home if you say it's time to go to bed? If you see your young child not cooperating in the classroom, know that you have some work to do at home.

WHAT KIND OF RULES?

Make sure you cover only the essentials. Don't come up with a long, overwhelming list. When I begin a class, I give the children four rules:

1 No talking unless you are called on.
2 Keep your hands to yourself, not on your neighbor.

3   No touching anything in the room.

4   Cooperate with the teacher and do everything asked.

Those are all the basic rules for the young classes. Younger children may not know the word "cooperate," but we give them an example, and they get it. We may have issues come up as we progress, and I'll give an explanation of how we will do something. But the basic rules don't change. Ever.

At home you need rules for a three-year-old that cover basic cooperation and safety. For example, in the car, your seatbelt has to be fastened. We don't throw our food. We don't hit. (And make sure you don't hit them.) We take a bath every day. Basics. Then enforce them with a reminder and an expectation that they follow through.

In the following examples, you can see my three Core Principles and my Six Steps to Sanity in action. It really can be done.

Prada, Jimmy Choo, Red Ruby Slippers...A Girl Has to Have Her Shoes

One day, I noticed a two-year-old whining at the classroom door, while her mother stood by, at a loss. As I approached, I asked the mother what the problem was.

She replied helplessly, "She wants to wear her party shoes to class, not the ballet slippers," as though all of her enrollment money was down the tubes, because her daughter wasn't allowed to wear the party shoes in the dance classroom—and clearly, her daughter had won the battle with her.

Fortunately, I had the Six Steps at my disposal. I slowed myself down and took a deep breath *(Step #1)*, and then, rather than moving right into a "These are the rules" lecture, I got curious about what was going on in Shelly's mind *(Step #2)*. I squatted down, breathed again, and smiled. "Hi Shelly," I said *(Step #3)*, "I'm Christine. What is the problem?" *(Step #4: Inquire candidly and respectfully, and really listen to the answer)*.

Shelly said, "I want to wear my party shoes."

I looked at her and said sincerely, "They are very pretty. I understand."

She smiled.

I went on, "At the dance studio we wear ballet slippers, and then after class kids can put on their favorite shoes." I spoke to her in a soft voice; anything louder is intimidating and off-putting. I did not talk in a high-pitched sing-song voice like many parents do with a two-year-old; I was conversing with an intelligent human being.

She got that and responded, "Okay. Mommy, hold my party shoes, and I'll wear them after class," (*Step #5: Discuss the situation with love, and decide on a course of action together*).

I said to Shelly, "Stop by after class and tell me how your dance class went," (*Step #6: Follow Up*).

That was it. No time was wasted with tears and drama and week after week of repeating the same fight. I simply treated Shelly like a human being (which her mother had failed to do, having assumed that she couldn't talk to her daughter reasonably) and followed my Six Steps to Sanity.

The mom was stunned and speechless.

Many a nonsensical mother would have argued, "What's the big deal? She's only two! Let her wear her party shoes. What difference does it make?!" These are the adults not seeing the big picture. You don't start teaching independence a month before college. Two is intelligent in my world. I'm not interested in chaos—I'm interested in a child learning to dance in her ballet slippers.

How Did It Get Late So Soon?

The most adorable little eight-year-old boy, Michael, showed up 15 minutes late to class. Of course, since he doesn't drive, it wasn't his fault. But it is my policy that if you are late, you observe class. It's important for the students and the parents to appreciate that the student must have a proper warm-up to prepare the body for class.

Additionally, being late—no matter what the reason—leads to all sorts of chaos, including others thinking it's okay to be late all the time, which becomes a distraction in class to those who care enough to be on time.

I needed to discuss the situation with Michael, so I used the Six Steps. First, I slowed down and took a deep breath (*Step #1*), and then I stopped the flood of old patterns and judgment, wiping any guesses I had as to why Michael was late from my mind (*Step #2*). "Hi, Michael," I said (*Step #3*), and asked, "What happened to cause you to be late?" (*Step #4: Inquire candidly and respectfully, and really listen to the answer*).

Michael replied, "We had to take my brother to karate, and the teacher wanted to talk to my mom about being late."

I responded, "Well, I'm sorry you are late. I was looking forward to you taking class, but these things can happen. I'd like you to observe and learn that way. I often find that students observing find out that they aren't the only ones who make mistakes, and you might see that while you watch today. Next week hopefully you can be here early. And I'll talk to your mom, too," (*Step #5: Discuss with love, and decide on a course of action together*).

He said okay. Kids know the drill. This was a life lesson being taught naturally through dance regarding the importance of preparation in life. I did follow up with Michael's mother, since he can't drive the car (*Step #6: Follow Up*).

Now, many a parent and teacher might feel tortured looking at "poor Michael" sitting alone being "punished" for the sins of his parents. And this is how we get tripped up: we can't see past the cuteness in the child, and out goes the life lesson in favor of "let's make an exception this one time," which always leads to another time, because the child will still be cute next week, and he didn't learn what he was or wasn't supposed to be doing.

I know. I've been there. I used to feel bad for "punishing" the student, so I would make an exception. But then, guess what? His parent would bring him late more and more. He always missed key instruction. So then I began enforcing my rule—but not with any sense of confidence. I'd have him sit and observe and secretly hope he wasn't going to hate me. Well, I never knew if he did or not because, BAM, here came the irate mom: "Why is Michael sitting there?! Are you punishing him? No, no no! Michael, come here. We are going home." Yikes.

Side note to dance parents: NEVER barge into a dance classroom or studio and make a scene. An inexperienced teacher will put up with it; an experienced studio owner will dismiss you from the studio under Sec. 2.4, Rule 12: "I offer dance lessons, not anger management."

These days, I look at the long term goal, even if that's just next week. I also function out of confidence. A dance student has to learn the rules of dance, and one of them is that you show up early—ideally 20 minutes early, to stretch, visit the bathroom, and socialize. You don't cruise in one minute before class. It's better for me to sit Michael down to observe—and there's enormous value from observing, by the way—and make sure that Michael and his parents get the message to get themselves organized and out the door early and respect the preparation of his body for the rigors of dance.

Some parents might think that enforcing this rule would be treating the child as less than a person, but truly, it's the opposite.

Teaching him now that rules are enforced shows that you care about him as a person, and that you respect his right to learn how to function as a real and whole person in society.

He will learn to expect that from himself and others. Independence comes from learning lessons and moving forward. He will learn from one well-handled consequence, and then you won't have to worry about dealing with the same problem over and over.

The key is to make and enforce rules *in conjunction with* follow-ing the Hanson Method. The Hanson method helps you create a connection with your child, so she will appreciate your rules and your efforts to help her develop as a person. Without the Hanson Method, you come off as controlling or bossy for no apparent reason.

ONLY THE PRINCE BRINGS CINDERELLA HER SLIPPERS

Here's another way that parents waste their time and miss out on teaching their children a valuable life lesson: their child shows up to the studio without her ballet slippers and the teacher won't let her take class without the shoes for safety reasons. What do you, the parent, do? If they arrived early, most parents would drive home and get the slippers and bring them back.

Loud game show buzzing sound

No. You are wasting your precious time. You take the conse-quences. Your child is not Cinderella; we're in the real world. Now, many would deem this cruel. I don't. If you have a child 6 or young-er, say that you forgot to put the shoes in the dance bag. Then say, "Next week will be better."

Children need to learn that there are consequences in life, and that no one—including you—is perfect.

If your child is 7 or older, say, "Next week, make sure you prepare your dance bag. You'll have to sit and watch today." Find the teachable moment, rather than venting helpless frustration or trying to be the hero. Be the hero by teaching.

Remember Core Principle Number 2: Your goal is to raise a whole and *independent* child. We need to give our children the opportunity to do things for themselves. Of course, if it had been a dress rehearsal or performance, yes, you would have needed to drive home and get the slippers. But for a weekly class, be grateful that a learning moment was provided, because if you go and get the slippers, the child learns that if she forgets something, someone else will cover for her.

Don't waste your time with bad training in your home, hoping that your child will magically do the right thing for you. You have to do the work. No child will do it for you. *Make rules and enforce them.* Kids are bright. They're ready to move on and test you on the next thing anyway.

TRUTH
+AMAZING

CHAPTER FIVE

CONSEQUENCES

It is my basic premise that all children are quite happy 97% of the time and can be peaceful and cooperative, given a loving and supportive environment. If you have less than that, it's time to restructure your approach—and that is what the majority of this book is about. But you do need a way to deal with that remaining 3%—when even the children in the best of environments behave poorly. This chapter will give you the tools you need for such times.

WHAT BEHAVIORS NEED TO BE ADDRESSED?

When deciding whether a particular behavior warrants correction, you have to walk a fine line between your own personal preference and genuinely harmful behavior. Ask yourself whether the behavior impinges on your child's health, safety, education, social welfare, or self improvement/independence.

If the behavior in question offends you simply because it is something you wouldn't do, then it is not really bad behavior. It is a personality choice.

For example, imagine a boy wanting to wear his hair in a spike. His parents may be more conservative, and would probably prefer that he chose a more traditional hairstyle. But wearing his hair in a spike is not bad, and his desire to do so does not require correction. If his school district does not allow it, then of course he should follow the rules they set, but he could spike his hair on the weekends.

At my dance studio, we require a sleeveless black leotard, but we do not require any specific style. The teenage girls have every black leotard style on the planet—criss-crossed, velvet, halter top, boat neck, etc. But if they wear long sleeves, they are reminded of the sleeveless policy; the sleeveless style allows us to see the line of the arm better. The next time they show up in such attire, they are asked to sit and observe. We don't make a federal issue out of it; we are quick to correct it without emotion.

HOW TO DEAL WITH LESS-THAN-IDEAL BEHAVIOR

When an unacceptable behavior comes up, you have to figure out fast what action needs to be taken. I have three main techniques that I recommend, depending on the situation: the Six Steps to Sanity, the Quick Reprimand, or the Two-Way Time-Out.

THE SIX STEPS TO SANITY™

The Six Steps to Sanity, which I introduced in Chapter 1, are my go-to technique. They are useful in many situations. For example, if a child is emotional—crying, arguing, refusing, fearful, unsure, etc.—the Six Steps can help you get to the reason for the extreme emotion. The Six Steps are also useful for a first time offense, because you can figure out the reason behind your child's actions, and you can then assist her. And the Six Steps are also essential when you need to deal with a behavior that is just downright unacceptable—a violation of safety or blatant disregard for a known rule. Such behavior is often indicative of a deeper problem, which is best discussed and dealt with together.

Harry Potter

A mom named Wanda came to me to talk about her eight-year-old daughter, saying, "Camille wants to read all of the Harry Potter books. I told her no. They're too mature for her and could give her nightmares." She continued, "It is annoying that she keeps coming back, begging me to let her read them."

I said, "Well, there is a reason she does that. Perhaps Camille senses your waffling. Are you unsure of your decision?" I asked.

"Yes, actually, I am," replied Wanda. "I know tons of kids way younger read the books and see the movies, and maybe I'm being too protective. But what if I guess wrong, and she can't sleep ever again?"

"Ah yes, the worries of a parent trying to do right. Sometimes we have to remove the need to be right when it's not obvious, and turn to *exploring* instead," I answered. "Parents are not always going to have the answer. In this case, Camille senses your indecision and pushes. If you continue to put off the decision, you open the door for her to decide. She can borrow the book from a friend or check it out at the library. The better route is to communicate with Camille exactly what you have shared with me. It's really a toss-up, because neither one of you has a magic 8 ball," I said.

Wanda's eyes were huge—a sure sign of an "Ah-ha" moment, as Oprah says.

"I'll do that. That sounds like the perfect plan," responded Wanda.

I followed up with Wanda and Camille a week later, and they had decided to read the books together, and talk about the scary parts openly when they came up. I checked in with them a month later, and they were still reading—and no nightmares. The Six Steps to Sanity helped Wanda and Camille communicate rationally and come to a mutual decision.

THE QUICK REPRIMAND™

The Quick Reprimand is just a "nip-it-in-the-bud" reminder of a basic rule that a child has previously demonstrated his under-standing of. It's great for public situations, or when time is of the essence. When the child complies, you just move on. I use this technique when a child knows better but is just caught up in another space—much like when parents start talking during a class observation, which is disrespectful to the students they are there to watch. The parents just get caught up in socializing. I don't need to use the Six Steps to Sanity in such cases; I just need to nip it in the bud quickly with something like, "Parents. Your quiet observation is needed."

Children are no different than parents. Someone starts a less than ideal behavior, and before you know it, more have joined in. A quick reminder makes all the difference.

Many parents are afraid to utilize the Quick Reprimand. Some are too angry, barking orders disrespectfully: "KIDS! Who do you think you are, yelling in a restaurant?!" Others are too submissive, looking on helplessly, or tentatively floating a suggestion: "It might be helpful to the other diners if we were all a little bit quieter and maybe didn't throw our food on the floor."

You and your child will be MUCH happier if you use the Quick Reprimand with alpha authority.

Be in charge. They will respect you for it.

Forgetting Their Manners

It was parent observation night in one of my other teachers' classes, and the costumes had just been handed out. The kids were buzzing with excitement and finding it hard to focus. When I walked in, several girls were talking over the teacher's instruction. (The teacher should not have allowed this; it is important to have consistency.)

As I passed them, I said, "Girls, what are you doing? Talking when a teacher is talking? Take your places for the beginning of the dance."

The quickness with which I spoke put them on high alert. They all knew the rules, so I didn't waste my time unnecessarily reviewing them.

Keep Your Emotions Out of It

Some parents think that if they don't deliver the correction with a bit of anger, it won't stick. Nothing is further from the truth. *Quickness is more effective and much healthier than anger.* If you deliver the news quickly and without emotion, you are sending a message to your child that you think she is intelligent enough to figure out a better route to take.

THE TWO-WAY TIME-OUT™

Sometimes young children's behavior is so over the top when they are sorting out the overwhelming speed of information they have to absorb, and adjustment or refocus is needed. In my experience, the most effective way to deal with such behavior is the practice commonly referred to as a "time-out"—but with a twist.

The key to an effective and non-damaging time-out is your mindset. A time-out *can* be used punitively—from the old parenting mindset of "I must punish bad behavior." But done well, it can serve as an opportunity for both you and your child to calm down, reflect, and get back to your normal set points.

The Time-Out

Time-outs are effective starting at age 2.

A time-out should always be carried out from the perspective of helping both of you calm down, NOT *out of a desire to punish.*

Simply ask your child (or direct him, as necessary) to sit somewhere close by. The time-out should last for one minute for every year of the child's age—and you should tell your child how long she needs to sit there. Tell her why she is in time-out *concisely*—in one sentence. And don't expect her to sit in a certain way, either. An upset child is not going to sit like she is at a wedding. It's better not to have an appointed place for the time-out; that way, when you are away from home and a time-out is necessary, you will be able to improvise. Do not put your child in time-out in a high traffic zone, where other people can stroll by to stare at the "bad kid." Respect your child's dignity. Neither should you make your child face the corner or sit in a dark or locked room. Such actions are punitive, which is not the point of the time-out.

The Twist

Most of the time, we think about time-outs as being for the child. In my world, the time-out serves both the child and the parent. Why? Because *you* may need to defuse so that you don't blow and go into your ineffective parenting style (which we'll cover in Chapter 7).

You need time to center yourself and get out of your head and into your heart, so that you can prepare yourself for using the Six Steps.

Children know right from wrong by age 5, and they don't misbehave unless you are being too controlling as a parent, or you have modeled inappropriate behavior. Children are so often punished for things they *learned by observing their own parents.* A child gets spanked by his parent and then hits someone at school. A parent yells at a child, but when the child yells at her sibling, she gets in trouble. Parents curse, and then punish their children for being rude to the teacher at school. *Use the time-out to think about where you went wrong.* Whether you sit with your child in silence, or in the next room, tell them that you, too, are going to reflect and/or calm down. Never turn down a chance to meditate.

The Close

When the two-way time-out is over, go to your child, take deep breaths, come down to his level, and *ask him in a soft voice if he knows why he was in time-out.* You don't need to go through the whole Six Steps, but you don't want him misunderstanding your intent. Yes, you told him at the beginning of the time-out, but sometimes in the heat of the moment children (much like adults) are not able to hear what you said. Perhaps during the two way time out you realize that you overreacted. Admit that. Do not nag, lecture, recap, or even teach about what your child did wrong. Later, you can go over it with the Six Steps.

Then *tell your child how much you love him,* and reiterate that it was the *behavior* that you didn't like, but that you love *him* always. "I didn't like your behavior when you threw your shoe at your little brother, *but I love you.*" Your child needs to know that your love for him is not dependent on his behavior.

Next, *have your child say "I'm sorry."* Apologizing has to be taught; we need to acknowledge the impact of our actions on others. Many adults still need to learn this skill. If your child is not inclined to say she's sorry because she doesn't think she did anything wrong, drop it until the next day. The more you use the Hanson Method, the more your child will own his behavior and want to apologize, because you're setting up a relationship based on mutual respect. Don't force her to say she's sorry by rote. It's meaningless to be on the receiving end of empty words. Teach your child that "I'm sorry" needs to be heartfelt.

Throughout the two-way time-out, be clear in your head that you are teaching your child, not punishing him.

Connect and humanize this intimate moment with a hug.

Ask, "May I give you a hug?" Kids of all ages like hugs. If he says yes, make it a good hug-- put your arms around your child, pull him towards you, and embrace him for a few seconds. Don't just pat him on the back like two basketball coaches at the end of a game. If your child is still upset and refuses the hug, you can say, "I understand. I love you," and go do something else and let him have his space.

A night's sleep always does wonders to reset us, doesn't it? If your child was still upset after the Two-Way Time-Out and didn't want to apologize or hug, take the first opportunity the next day to invite your child to sit with you, and use the Six Steps to talk it out. Who knows, maybe you'll discover that you were actually the one who needed to apologize.

To reinforce the lesson that your child learned, make it the theme of the week. Do not focus on what he did wrong, and by all means, do not lecture about it, but find happy, conversational ways to focus on the benefits of engaging in the better, alternative behavior.

The 3-Year-Old and the Motorcycle

My 3-year-old grandson accompanied me to a local pizzeria. As we walked in the door, we could see an area off to the side with the bright lights of a game arcade flashing. My grandson saw a motorcycle in front of a video screen, and that's where he wanted to go. He was content to pretend to drive the motorcycle, too young to realize that the flashing screen was prompting us to insert coins, so we played on it for a while. Then we went to eat our pizza, returning afterwards for some more motorcycle fun. Soon it was near his bed time, and we needed to head home.

Little did I realize that we would be experiencing his first meltdown. When I announced it was time to go, he burst into tears, yelling and holding his body rigid in protest.

Caught by surprise, but still calm, I confidently stated, "If you don't leave the bike now, we are going to miss bedtime."

He didn't get off the bike. The Quick Reprimand had fallen on deaf ears, and the situation certainly wasn't right for the Six Steps to Sanity. I knew a Two-Way Time-Out was on the horizon, but an arcade was not the place for it, and he was getting tired.

I continued in a calm, loving, but firm voice, "If you don't come off of the bike, I will pick you up and carry you to the car seat, and when we get home we will have a 3-minute time-out to think about all of this. I will count to 3, and by the count of 3, you have to be off of the motorcycle. One – two – three."

He didn't move.

I followed through with what I said I would do, without saying a word. He wailed on the way home. That's okay. When we got home, I sat him in a chair for three minutes. He was still mad, so he slumped down in the chair with a bit of a pout. I went to the adjacent room, leaving the door open, to collect myself and get out of my head and into my heart. I only had three minutes, so deep breaths were essential.

After our time-out, I took some more deep breaths, squatted down next to his chair, and asked him why we had taken a time out.

He said, "Because I didn't want to leave the motorcycle."

I realized that he had "reset," so it was a good time to talk about what had gone wrong. I had now had some time to think through the situation, and I had figured out that I had mishandled our exit. I was candid with him about it, saying, "Instead of giving you a warning first that we would be leaving, I just said, 'We're going now.' You were having fun, and it wasn't nice of me to just say, "Let's go," without giving you some time to say good-bye to the motorcycle. I was thinking about getting you to bed, but I could have given you some warning, like 'In 5 minutes we are going.' Then you could have played hard for those 5 minutes. After that, I should have said, 'In 1 minute we have to say good-bye to the motorcycle until the next time we come back.' That would have been more respectful to you."

His eyes lit up, and the energy returned to his limp body. He was feeling respected and hopeful that this wouldn't happen again. He sat up and said, "I like that, Nani."

I said, "So do I. That's what we're going to do when we go back to the pizza place. But now, I want to say I'm sorry, because I am really sorry you had to go through not having time to say bye to the motorcycle."

He said promptly, "I'm sorry to for getting mad."

We were both smiling and giving the biggest of hugs to each other. We happily got ready for bed.

The next day at breakfast, while we were playing with toy cars, I mentioned again that the next time we went the pizza place with the motorcycle, I would give him a lot of notice, such as a 10-minute, 5-minute, and 1-minute countdown, so he could prepare himself. I went over this a couple more days, and then we went back just to play on the motorcycle. It all went smoothly.

My grandson knew that if I said something, I'd follow through. A couple more times I had to use the "One-Two-Three" announcement that would lead to a time-out, but I never got to three. He would always cooperate, remembering that one time-out. By age 5, he never needed a time out again.

When you use the Two-Way Time-Out and the Six Steps to Sanity, you will often discover that *you* were the instigator of the problem.

In my experience, a meltdown, regardless of the child's age, is ALWAYS a reaction to an ineffective parenting move.

Don't blame behavior problems on your child. Get moving with the Hanson Method.

I highly recommend the countdown announcement to help your child transition to a new activity, such as brushing her teeth and getting ready for bed or leaving the house to go to dance class. I can hear parents saying, "Yeah, right—I'm gonna do all that. They can get their butts in gear when I say so." But please remember that your child is not your prisoner. That kind of attitude will only earn their disrespect.

In the theater, a page goes around to all the dressing rooms announcing, "Fifteen minutes to places, everyone," and the actors all respond, "Thank you." Later, they announce, "Places, everyone. Five minutes to curtain." Why do they do this? Because people like to know what's coming. It's respectful, and it allows the performers a smooth transition to what they have to do next. You can afford your child the same courtesy.

I strongly feel that if you are engaged in the Hanson Method, teaching and learning with the use of the Six Steps to Sanity, one or two time-outs in every 4-month period for two-, three-, and four-year-olds is pretty much all you need. By age five, you probably won't even need time-outs at all anymore.

Through the Teen Years

Over-the-top teen moments, quite frankly, won't come up if you've been consistently implementing the techniques presented here. If you've been respecting your child, you won't get the "typical" teenage misbehaviors of talking the parent down, rebelling, eye rolling/huffing, or worse. These behaviors are the result of a disconnect between parents and their children. With my methods, these behaviors just won't happen. I include these measures here, though, for parents who are just starting out with my techniques and need some way of addressing the outbursts that they're still experiencing with their teens.

You can continue using Two-Way Time-Outs into your child's adolescence. If you're the parent of an older child just starting my techniques, you my feel uncomfortable imposing a time-out on a teenager; maybe you wish your teen just wouldn't mess up. But the burden is on you to guide her. And just because she may be taller than you—or smarter—neither of you gets a pass. You will see results from my techniques quickly, if you stay with them.

In the teen years, your child's bad behavior may seem more flagrant to you, but it is usually age appropriate. For example, a two-year-old may have a meltdown over not getting candy in the grocery store; a teen may stomp, pout, glare, and/or declare, "You're mean! Every other parent at the entire school is letting their kid go to the [unsupervised] lake party!"

A two way time-out is in order. Many parents make the mistake of countering such an over-the-top and disrespectful comment, explaining why exactly they are not mean. But it's much better to realize that such behavior is not to be tolerated for your sake *or for the teen's sake.* As with a two-year-old, talk *after* the time-out. Resist the urge to dictate or plead your side of the case for now.

If your child is 16, he will have a 16-minute time-out, during which time he can reflect and will probably realize he was out of line, exaggerating, dramatic, embellishing, etc. These are normal teenage feelings; you still have to stick to the rules that you have set for his teenage safety. Whatever you do, don't forget the last part of the Two-Way Time-Out. The Close is the most important part.

Take some deep breaths and pull up a chair next to your child for eye-to-eye contact. In a soft voice, ask why you both had a time-out. With tweens and teens, you can share your reasons, too, but let your child go first so she can learn how to reflect and figure out her part in the problem—another skill many adults lack. Train her now. You might hear something like, "I was rude to you, and I was yelling and acting all crazy." Then you can share, "For me, it's important not to allow people to call me names. Also, my priority is to think about your safety." Tell her that you love her. "I didn't like the outburst, but *I love you*." And don't forget the apology and the hug. If you've been using the Hanson Method, your teen or tween will probably offer up an apology freely, but if not, you can say, "Is there anything you would like to say?" Then hug it out, and keep in mind that teens doth protest too much. They love hugs from their parents, so if she says, "Nah I'm good," you could try something like, "Well, I need a hug! Can I get one?" I would say that 99% of the time, if your child is over being mad, she will be secretly grateful for a hug.

Here's something important to know. If your child is usually very cooperative and this teen explosion has come out of the blue, you may discover during the Six Steps that he doesn't really *want* to go to the lake party at all! That's right. He may have subconsciously created the drama just so he'd get to the time-out and the Six Steps to process how he feels and what action he wants to take. He may have felt torn between being a "regular" teen and not knowing how to deal with party pressures to drink, smoke, do drugs, or dance intimately. The Two-Way Time-Out, used consistently over the years, will actually prime the pump for the Six Steps.

INAPPROPRIATE CONSEQUENCES

When children do something "wrong," we often react emotionally and punish them accordingly. If your goal is to facilitate your child's growth to wholeness and independence, this type of punishment is not only largely ineffective, but it is also detrimental. I want to make clear the types of consequences that have *no* place in your parenting repertoire. Whether the chosen form of punishment is spanking, physical restraint, rough handling, disparaging words, silent treatment, abandonment, taking their things away, or grounding, it all leaves deep scars. This is unacceptable.

CORPORAL PUNISHMENT

Physical punishment (spanking, physical restraint, or rough handling) and verbal attacks (disparaging words, yelling) instill fear, not to mention being a bad example of how to act toward others.

Aggressive behavior, physical or verbal, results in children with bullying issues.

To be clear, my definition of spanking includes everything from the use of a belt or other object to a swat on the butt or a smack on the hand. In the long term, it doesn't work, and it causes emotional harm.

I am stunned and amazed at the number of parents who believe in spanking. Once again, no critical thinking is being applied here at all. They truly are only doing it because their parents did it to them. Parents attempt to justify spanking with comments such as, "Oh, I only spanked her until she was four," "That's what kept me in line," or "I just slapped her hand, and she needed it."

We have advanced so much as a society: women have the right to vote; people everywhere advocate equal pay for equal work; PETA fights against animal abuse. So why is it still okay to beat, hit, spank, or slap an innocent child? It's certainly not effective: the child will repeat the offending behavior. *Spanking is not okay.* It's the ultimate in bullying—and then our society wonders why we have so many bullies in our schools. There you go. I want to make this clear: you don't play at using the Hanson Method, and then resort to spanking when you are losing it. That approach won't work, and it's not right. Spanking is barbaric, and one day our society will look at having sanctioned it as sheer insanity.

EMOTIONAL PUNISHMENT

Silent treatment and abandonment both victimize your child's emotions, without teaching her anything.

Silent treatment means actively withholding communication with your child as a punishment, usually without explanation or indication of an ending time. (I'm not talking about a time-out, which can be handled in a loving and respectful way.) Abandonment means leaving your child alone out of anger, without telling him where you are going or when you'll be back. This includes actions like getting in the car and driving around the corner to scare your 6-year-old into hurrying up when you say "get ready."

TAKING AWAY YOUR CHILD'S THINGS

Taking away necessities or things that are good for your children's growth sends your child a schizophrenic message: that you don't find value in the things you otherwise tell them are of value. I'm talking about food, shelter, and love, of course, but I'm also talking about things like planned trips, visits with family, extracurricular activities, toys, TV, video games, playtime with friends, movies, etc.

Your goal is not to evoke anguish in your child in return for her misbehavior.

Do not make your decisions about appropriate consequences based on how much your child enjoys a certain activity.

If your spouse enjoys golf or running, you wouldn't take away his/her golf clubs or running shoes to get to get his/her attention when you're having a disagreement, would you? In fact, your spouse may very well need the golf or the running to deal with the argument. It's the same for your child.

> *Allow him to process his misbehavior without disrupting other parts of his life.*

If you use the Six Steps to Sanity, the Quick Reprimand, and the occasional Two Way Time-Out, you will not need to take away items and activities that your child enjoys.

An extension of this idea is throwing away your child's things, either because you are fed up with them, or you think it will get your child's attention. Never do that. Whether your child is melting down over a melting ice cream cone, or simply has a toy he never uses, it is *his* food and *his* toy. Throwing it away is completely disregarding your child as a person. Would you get upset at a friend and go to her house and take back the toaster you bought her for a wedding gift? Would you throw away that vase she never uses while you're over at her house having coffee? Of course not. If the issue is a meltdown, you now have the tools to deal with it. If the toy count is getting out of control at your house, then clean the closet out together, with sorting goals in mind. Above all, treat your child *and his things* with respect.

GROUNDING

Unless your child has been convicted by a federal court for hacking into a government computer or evading taxes on her online business bonanza, grounding is not a good idea. Why? It's house arrest-- a punishment used to penalize criminals. If your child is a criminal, turn her into the local police station. Otherwise, use the Six Steps to Sanity and get to the root of the problem and effect healing.

It is okay to be upset about a child's misbehavior. It is *not* okay to lash out and try to make your child upset in return. Do not punish. Your child might try to mask her resulting fear, sadness, and anger. She may even act like she can handle the punishment you're dishing out. But the punishments described above dry up a bit of your child's wholeness, and the repercussions will surface, as she turns to negative experiences in a vain attempt to heal the withered parts of her soul.

You Did What?!

I had dismissed a class for a water break, and a mother starting chatting me up. Out of the blue, she told me that she was working with her eight-year-old daughter, Janna, to help her be less lazy in life. She wanted Janna to practice dance more, clean her room, pick up the dog's messes in the backyard, and take more initiative in general. She told me I should see an improvement.

I had no complaints about Janna—she was sweet, cooperative, and very energized in her dance. She tended to be unsure of herself and needed a lot of encouragement, but she would rise to the occasion when asked.

Imagine my shock when the mother continued, "Whenever I see her slacking off or being lazy, I get the belt out and spank her with it until she shows some fire."

I was stunned into silence.

By age 10, Janna had become a shell of her youthful self: quiet, withdrawn, and plagued by invented injuries. By age 15, she was a bully.

This is what I want to shout from the rooftops...

> ... the punishments that parents think will correct a child result in behavior that is often worse than the behavior the parents were trying to correct in the first place!

Sometimes parents need to correct a child for hitting someone, so they beat the child to teach him a lesson. In this case, the mother didn't like laziness, but the punishment she dished out killed her daughter's inborn energetic spirit, and she became withdrawn. Later, the daughter did deliver some of the initiative her mother was looking for, but in the form of bullying.

It's Never What the Parent Thinks

One of my teachers came rushing into my office, where I was talking to an assistant. For her to interrupt me, I knew it was something major.

She exclaimed, "Christine, I am teaching class, and all of a sudden Zoey, in the MIDDLE of a combination, just starts flailing her arms about like a comedian. I gave her our usual 30-second time-out,[3] and then Adam started doing the same thing, and now *he's* in time out, and they're both laughing. I've never experienced this—and they know better. I'm sending them to you immediately."

I only had 15 minutes before I had to teach, so I had to go through the Six Steps with both kids together. I slowed myself down and took a deep breath (*Step #1*). Then I cleared my mind of any ideas that were popping up as to why these two were misbehaving (*Step #2*) I greeted Zoey and Adam (*Step #3*), both age 8, in a soft voice, and I invited them to sit in the same oversized chair across from my desk. I said, "Hey, your teacher tells me that you were throwing your arms around in the middle of a ballet combination and laughing about it. I am wondering why?" (*Step #4: Inquire candidly and respectfully, and really listen to the answer*).

Zoey immediately answered, "I don't know."

I offered my standard phrase for such situations: "Well, I know that when someone *says* they don't know, they really *do* know but they feel uncomfortable saying anything. You can tell me the truth."

So she said, "I was bored."

I looked at Adam, and he said, "Like she said. I was bored."

---

[3] Please note that institutional consequences are different from the types of consequences that parents should utilize. Your goal as a parent is to keep your connection with your child strong so that you can facilitate his growth into a whole and independent person. Institutional goals are different. In the case of our dance studio, our goal is to provide an environment in which all students can learn and practice dance—and time is always of the essence. Thus, you may notice that the ways we handle disruptions are different from the methods I advocate you use as a parent.

(Step #5: Discuss with love and decide on a course of action together.) I asked, "Well, if it's boring, then why didn't you choose to do the more fun class in the other classroom?"

Zoey replied, "I like the challenges in this one."

Adam echoed, "Yeah, I like the challenges."

I said to Adam, who so far had just been parroting Zoey, "That's interesting. I'm curious. How far do you want to go in dance? To what level?"

He said, "To Ballet V," (our highest level).

Zoey said, "I want to go as far as I can go in dance."

Treating Zoey and Adam with great respect, as though we were in a business meeting, I said, "With that in mind, have you ever watched the advanced ballet classes?"

Neither one had.

I went on, "If you had to guess, do you think that those students do goofy things? Or are they quiet and focused?"

They both said, "Quiet and focused."

I asked, "Why is that important?"

Adam replied, "Well, you aren't going to be able to focus if you're thinking of your next funny move."

"Well said. I agree," I said. "I have to go teach now, but I want you to understand that when you goof off, you hurt your teacher who works so hard to make you great, and you hurt you. I think you both need to apologize to your ballet teacher."

They agreed.

I said, "I want to hear back from you both after your next ballet class to tell me how it went, and how you felt with your new decisions," *(Step #6: Follow Up)*.

I went to teach my class.

When I was done, Zoey's mom, Stella, was waiting for me. I invited her into my office to talk, and she asked, "Well, what has Zoey done this time?"

I asked her why she'd phrased it that way.

She replied, "Oh, because Zoey keeps back-talking everybody."

I countered, "She doesn't back talk me."

Stella said, "Well, everyone else. I remember when you talked to her last year when I said she was having trouble at school, and that really helped a lot. But lately she just doesn't care."

I said, "Yes, the ballet teacher said she was very nonchalant. With me she was still in a silly mood at the beginning of our talk. I'm curious. How is it you knew she was in trouble at school?"

Stella answered, "Zoey would get in the car and say Mrs. Martin, her music teacher, was mean. So I went and talked to Mrs. Martin, who told me Zoey acts reckless and doesn't care if she gets in trouble."

I asked, "How do you correct her smart-aleck remarks at home?"

She said, "Oh, I tell her to watch her mouth. Sometimes I get my husband involved, and he spanks her."

There it was. It's always punishment and the child-as-prisoner mentality that leads to this stuff.

I said, "In my world, punishment is something we don't do to children. Spanking is one of those things."

She countered, "Oh, I mean, it's just three swats, and it doesn't even hurt."

I said, "To you. To Zoey, I'm sure it does. There's not any reason it wouldn't hurt her and her feelings."

Stella protested, "But if we don't do that, what are we going to do?! I've taken away Xbox, TV, everything. I don't want to take away dance, because I pay too much for it."

I said, "Yes, dance is education, so that's not to be taken away. There are many things to do, and the second I get my book done, you might consider reading it. Until that time, let me give you a crash course." I quickly outlined the Hanson Method and the Six Steps to Sanity. "Communication always trumps punishment," I explained.

Stella was listening with tears running down her face—I had hit a nerve.

I continued, "I suspect that you did the punishment because you didn't know of anything better to do. But if you step back, you'll see that spanking and taking things away has had no impact on her behavior, right?"

She nodded.

"I'm going to ask you to step out, and I want to talk to Zoey," I said.

Zoey came into my office, and I sat on the floor with her and dimmed the lights. I began the Six Steps, slowing myself down and taking deep breaths *(Step #1)*. I cleared my head as much as I could, because at this point I thought I knew what was going on—but I had to remain open to new discoveries *(Step #2)*.

I smiled, and said, "Hi again, Zoey," *(Step #3)*. "I just talked to Mom, and now let me ask you: what is the hardest thing about the parenting in your house?" *(Step #4: Inquire candidly and respectfully, and really listen to the answer)*.

She said, "When I smart off, I have to hear 'Bite your tongue.'"

I said, "Is there anything else?"

She shook her head no.

I asked, "How do you feel about the spankings?"

She looked incredibly sad and vulnerable. In a soft voice, she said, "I don't like them. But Dad doesn't do them like his dad. His dad used a belt, and my dad just uses his hand, so that is better."

I'm always amazed how parents can put a spin on the punishments they dole out. Zoey believed the hype.

I looked Zoey in the eyes and said, "I don't think so. To me, it's not okay to ever spank a child. If it happened to me, I'd feel very sad and hurt."

She continued, "Sometimes when I know that Mom has sent Dad to spank me, I run and jump in bed and pretend to be asleep to get out of it." Then she just looked at me, and we sat in silence for a moment. Finally, she said, "I do feel sad."

I said, "I bet. Question for you. I'm sure you know that you're going to get in trouble when you smart back to your parents but you go ahead and do it anyway. Would you say there's a part of you that just can't resist?"

She nodded vigorously.

I asked the obvious. "Do you feel mad at your parents sometimes?"

She did the biggest nod of the head I've ever seen. "Yes!"

I told Zoey I was going to bring mom in.

Stella came in, and I asked her to join us on the floor. At first, Zoey hung her head and drew circles on the carpet while I talked, still in a soft voice. "Zoey and I had a great conversation, and she's a brave girl to share so much. I have a saying that these kids are smarter than the adults. They are super wise and mature. Zoey doesn't like to misbehave—it's just that because of the spankings, she's down on herself. She feels sad and mad when the spankings happen, and it leaves her asking herself, 'Why should I bother when the people I love the most hurt me?' So she has a flippant, 'I-don't-care' attitude. But she *does* care. She wants to do well at school and dance and at home," I said.

Stella had tears rolling down her face again. Zoey peeked up at her mom.

I continued, "The spankings need to stop. Communication needs to be used. It will be hard at first."

Stella said, "Yeah, it is just automatic. That's all I think of, is yelling at her or getting my husband to be the heavy."

I said, "Yes, and you're both complicit. He does the spankings, but you sanction it. And you yell at her. That's why she pushes against both of you. I understand how as parents we think we should do it the same way our parents did, or we think, "Hey, I survived it." But if we really reach deep, we know we have issues, and we don't like them. This is about doing the best for our kids."

I turned to Zoey and told her, "Zoey, if you feel that Mom and Dad are slipping into old ways, just remind them in a polite way so that you can take care of you." I wanted to give Zoey a tool to use, because I suspected Mom was going to struggle with the change— plus she had to get her husband onboard as well, and he wasn't at our get-together.

To Stella, I said, "Zoey was really brave to look inside herself and be honest. I appreciate that you did the same. A whole bunch of mothers in the same boat would have been cursing me and jerking their child out the door and slamming it behind them. They could not have handled the truth. You have the courage to hear all of this and be open in front of Zoey. And this is where the healing starts. I promise you that if you treat her with respect, using communication instead of punishment, you will have great breakthroughs. And if Zoey slips up, give yourselves both a time-out; you use the time-out not to figure out a punishment, but to center yourself and get out of your mind and into your heart, so you can communicate," (*Step #5: Discuss with love, and decide on a course of action together*).

At this point, Zoey was snuggled up to her mom, and Stella had her arm around her. The moment was warm, tender, and raw all at the same time. There was work to be done in their home, but now that the secrets were out, they could work on the real issues, instead of tip-toeing around mine fields and complaining about the child.

I gave them both huge hugs and told them each how proud I was of them. Stella thanked me profusely, and off they went. I will continue to check in with them and ask how they're doing over the next few weeks and months (*Step #6: Follow Up*).

You can see in this story how Zoey had been damaged by her parents' punishment, and the part of her spirit that had dried up was seeking out unhealthy situations in order to heal itself. She felt like less than a person, having been treated with disregard by the parents she loves dearly, so she had no regard for herself and her goals. Her self pride had dried up, so she kept recreating behavior she couldn't be proud of. She back-talked to academic teachers and acted goofy in dance – in a class she adores. This kept her stuck in a cycle of being unable to be proud of herself. She talked back to her parents, because it was her only way to push back against them. She couldn't physically stop them. They disrespected her; she did the same in return—part modeled and learned, part biological fight response.

Out Comes the "S" Word

Beatrice is a spirited and gifted child, but in this story, we will see how she switched up into something aggressive.

We were in a dance class, and there were two groups each making up a bit of choreography very quickly for a project. One group was trying to get the last girl, Karen, to pick up the new steps, and all of them were talking at once. Karen was confused, asking if she had the step correct. Suddenly, Beatrice lunged towards her with an emphatic chop of her hand and yelled, "Shut-up!"

This was highly unusual behavior for Beatrice, and using the Quick Reprimand, I stated, loudly enough to be heard over the hubbub, "We do not use that word!"

We continued on with class, and since it got out late in the evening, I waited until the next day to use my Six Steps to Sanity to discuss the incident with Beatrice, knowing that a good night's sleep would help both of us be fresh for our talk.

The next day, I called her into my office. I slowed myself down and took some deep breaths *(Step #1)*, and I cleared my head of any thoughts about Beatrice's actions. *(Step #2)* I pulled up a chair so that we were face-to-face. In a soft voice, I greeted Beatrice *(Step #3)*. "Hey, Beatrice," I said. "I need to discuss yesterday, when you told Karen to shut up. That was an aggressive act and was actually bullying," *(Step #4: Inquire candidly and respectfully, and really listen to the answer)*.

She looked embarrassed, but at the same time, she looked like she didn't get it.

I went on, "In my world, 'shut-up' is a put-down to another person. It sends a message that what they have to say doesn't matter. That's bullying. If I were Karen I would have felt sad."

In denial, Beatrice said, "Well, I was actually saying it to the whole group."

I said, "I saw the entire thing, and you were clearly saying it only to Karen. Besides, even if you had said it to the whole group, it still would have been inappropriate."

Beatrice flip-flopped, saying, "Well she didn't seem to be depressed afterwards."

"Beatrice, whether she had a reaction or not does not make it okay for you to do what you did. Just because you didn't see her sad, doesn't mean that it didn't hurt and embarrass her. Do you understand that?" I said, as softly as I could.

She circled back around, searching for a palatable answer. "I just wanted the whole group to get it right," she said.

Now, instead of arguing that she hadn't addressed her comment to the whole group, I picked up on this new bit of information that was possibly driving her inappropriate behavior. I said, "That is interesting. Why was it necessary to get it right?"

Bam. We had gone deep enough to hit a nerve. Now Beatrice was sobbing, saying, "There's just all this pressure and pressure to get it right."

Softly, I asked, "What pressure, Beatrice?"

"Just, like, in school to get good grades, " she said. Now we had strayed from the incident I had called her in for, but I kept following her lead.

"Who puts the pressure on you for the grades?" I asked.

She cried some more and said, "I do. I never had homework, and now I do. And it's hard because I have homework after school and go to dance *and* I'm supposed to practice flute, and then more homework, and try to get to sleep."

At this point in the sobbing, many adults would hug the child or stop the conversation, but crying is not a bad thing. She was feeling something, and that juices our dried parts back into life.

I asked, "Do you think the homework is too much? Can you handle it, or do you need a tutor?" Through tears, she said, "No. I can do it. I can learn. I'm just behind my peers."

"Do you think you need to back off of dance or getting good grades?" I asked, so that she could get clear on her intentions in life.

She replied, "No, I can do both well. I *want* to do both well, for me."

I said, "And with that goal in mind, I know you will achieve it. Is there anything else you'd like to share?"

She said, "I'm just sorry I did that to Karen."

"Beatrice, I'm so happy you said that. I think you owe her an apology. What do you think?" I asked.

"I think so, too," she said.

"Okay, we can all talk tomorrow," *(Step 6: Follow Up)*. I gave her a hug, and she disposed of her wet tissues. As she walked out the door, I said, "I think you showed a great deal of bravery and maturity in this conversation. I like that about you."

I called her mom, Georgia, as her dad was picking her up. Upon hearing the news, Georgia acknowledged that her behavior was very serious, and that she was "going to punish" Beatrice by not allowing her to go to a dance conference that she had been looking forward to for over 3 months.

I told Georgia that if she had been in my office, she would have witnessed how Beatrice's ability to understand some buried part of herself, in addition to finally seeing the error of her ways, had been more productive than any punishment. I briefly explained that I don't believe in punishment, and I advised her to just talk to her daughter.

One week later, Georgia came to me to talk about the incident, and I understood where Beatrice had gotten her ability to deflect rather than own up to her actions. Georgia said, "You know, girls are so competitive today, and that can lead to bullying. I read that on a bullying website."

I said, "I don't agree."

She continued, "Well, it can also be friends doing it to them that causes it."

I said, "I still don't agree. It starts in the home."

There was a pause. Then Georgia said, "Oh, but I think a close friend can bully, and then Beatrice thinks it's okay."

I continued, "Actually, I still disagree. It starts in the home with the parents. Beatrice said, "Shut-up," because she was intolerant of imperfection. That most likely means one of you at home is intolerant of imperfection. Then you couple that with her punishments over the years. Punishment is bullying. It's a math equation. One plus one equals the apple not falling far from the tree."

Georgia softly replied, "I think you're right."

Now, I have to give kudos to Georgia for being the type of parent who can even hear any of this. Many a parent would have verbally attacked me—a kill the messenger sort of thing. Georgia took it in.

I went on, "If Beatrice allowed herself the vulnerability to get to a healing place, so can you. If, as a parent, you have resorted to punishment or lecturing out of knee-jerk frustration, you have successfully trained Beatrice to resort to the same when she is equally frustrated, and she too wants someone to 'get it right,' a.k.a. be perfect. She will also develop denial strategies to prevent herself from readily accepting her misbehavior. If she knows she'll be punished, a smart thing is to deny any wrongdoing ever happened. It becomes habit to pretend at perfection and blame the misbehavior on something—or someone—else. That will be the pressure cooker she feels that she's in. Let go of punishment, for starters, and let in communication. That alone is enormously healing. Her pressure cooker state will be lifted. She'll know that communication is an option, rather than fearing the next round of punishment."

Georgia was in such a vulnerable place. She said, "I have to go to her right now and talk to her about my part in all of this. And we as her parents looked the other way for years when our friend's daughter bullied her, and we told her to ignore it, or that she could deal with it. Bad choice. I get that now. Even though the girls were friends, we were complicit in her victimization."

I agreed. I added, "Beatrice will most likely defend you and say that you had nothing to do with her bullying. Don't agree with her."

After Georgia and I talked, I realized that she, too, had been in denial, scouring the internet to come up with reasons for her daughter's bullying. It's very hard for parents to accept responsibility.

Later, I got an email that the two of them had had a beautiful and productive conversation. Beatrice had indeed defended her mother, saying that she had done no wrong (more denial), and that she, Beatrice, deserved all the blame. But Georgia stayed with her and owned her part.

The bottom line is this...

> *If you engage in these types of punishment, you—one of the people your child loves the most in the world—are engaging in the same behavior used by governments to break prisoners.*

You are setting your own child up for emotional issues. Please. Stop. Now.

WHY WE PUNISH

We punish our children because we are bewildered, split in half.

> *We were treated with disrespect as children, and now we've grown into adults with the dried up bits of ourselves still there.*

As I've mentioned, these dried up parts will seek to be whole, but they ineffectively seek out like energy: negative attracts negative. A part of us wants love; the other part believes love will never happen to us.

This negative part inside of us pops up at the least convenient times, but we have hindsight to give us an opportunity to choose differently and to heal. Half the time we love our kids, and half the time we think we are ruining them. We're right.

Mt. Vesuvius

A volcano eruption, as described by eHow contributor S.F. Heron, bears remarkable similarities to some "parenting" I've seen.

"Some volcanoes," Heron writes, "Erupt quietly; others violently shoot gas, steam and ash into the air." Not all volcanoes release their pressure in the classic style—by exploding. Similarly, parents dishing out punishments to their children may appear "calm," but this quiet belies the pressure building up inside them. This kind of pressure builds up for various reasons: exhaustion, stress, hunger, confusion, or frustration, to name a few. And it comes from the DUBOOs inside that wants to heal.

Heron goes on to describe the effects of the volcano on its surroundings:

Every volcano makes a change to the landscape of the earth after an eruption. Volcanoes build new earth with every eruption, spewing hot lava from deep inside the earth onto the much cooler surface. After a volcano erupts, the magma flows down the sides of the volcano, reaching a point where it cools enough to stop flowing.

As the flow progresses, everything in the lava's path is consumed. Plants, animals, buildings, roads, and trees are burned completely. Lava flows cool over time and forms new rock. Wind, rain, and water after lava flows with weathering to break down lava and turn it into soil.

Indeed, when parents erupt—violently or not—it damages their children. Not sometimes. Always. Did you notice that the magma flows down until "reaching a point where it cools enough to stop flowing?" That is what punishing is about. Until the parent has released his internal aggression, he can't stop punishing his child. The need to release the burning lava that burns him up inside will scorch his child each and every time.

Whether parents say so or not, I think they all hate the spanking and punishing, but they don't know what else to do. They've never seen effective parenting, because it is so seldom witnessed. So they go along with the herd mentality: "If everyone else is doing it, and they've been doing it for years, it must be the appropriate thing to do."

Do we want to raise our children to be as damaged and ineffective as we are? Of course not. But it's hard to come up with a better game plan while you are in the trenches. That's why I wrote this book.

The Hanson Method is simple, and it produces positive change very quickly, with the added benefit of healing you, too.

So don't punish. Teach.

THE TRUTH ABUU
A SIMPLE GUIDE TO TRANSFORMIN

You know wh
times parentir
really suppos
We want our
and we want
But how?

CHAPTER SIX

CHALLENGES

If you thought this chapter was going to be about the challenges of parenting...sorry! I've peppered those throughout the entire book. This chapter is about facilitating your child's growth to independence through fun challenges you undertake together. In the process, they will feel your love for them pouring forth, and they will love you back for it.

Remembering that your child is a human being—and a super cool one at that—gives rise to a kind of love and enthusiasm that you won't have to fake.

Do you really engage with your child?

> *You have a magnificent opportunity to experience enormous, wholehearted love with your child and learn about each other as you BOTH grow.*

You will reap rewards beyond your imagination as you fan the flame of your love for each other.

QUICK REVIEW

Just to recap the previous chapters:

1 Adopt the Hanson Parenting Mindset. Wake up. Throw out your parents' model. *Your child is a person.* Respect his choices. Raise him to be *whole* and *independent.*
2 Act out of *love* and *positivity.*
3 Create, communicate, and enforce the basics, but *ban the idea of "punishment" from your mind.*
4 Use the *Six Steps to Sanity* to resolve conflict and discover issues.
5 Use a Two-Way Time-Out if things get heated and at least one of you is not in your natural, pleasant state.

FLIP FLOP: CHALLENGE YOUR CHILD

Whenever I need to inspire my dance students or acknowledge them for doing a great job, I give them a challenge, and they love it. For example, when my five-year-old acrobatic students master a forward roll, I say, "Hmm. The older kids do a run and then a forward roll. Let's do it." Or, for the six- and seven- year olds who tend to find ballet "boring," I reinvented how their class is taught at my studio, calling it Pre-Beginning Ballet Survivor Island. For everything they do exceedingly well, they must do a challenge, which is something best described as a ballet obstacle course. This is met with the highest level of excitement children can exhibit without actually exploding out of their skin. They all leave class asking their parents how many days until they get to come back for ballet.

A challenge is a thoughtful mini-adventure into something age- or person-appropriate. (Notice I added "person-appropriate." The person is really more important than the age. I have a four-year-old in my studio who can read college text books; but of course not every four-year-old reads, let alone wants to do phonics. Some kids are interested in animals, others love cars or ponies or ice-skating. It just depends on the person.) The challenge can be something you introduce and then watch the child do by himself, or it can be something you do together. Either way, you are sending the message, "I know you are smart, and here's something else I trust that you can learn."

So many adults try to baby or control children. But if you work towards inspiring them, and expanding their horizons, and you will have much happier children. Flip flop your energies.

Instead of paying so much attention to the BAD—the bad behavior, the bad things that COULD happen—introduce challenges.

Take off the negative glasses and focus on the positive to stimulate teaching, independence and appreciation.

The Chicken or the Egg

One day, when my grandson was three, I was making him some scrambled eggs. I could see how frustrating it must be from his perspective not to be part of the process. Heck, all that action up on that big, mysterious stove, and he couldn't see any of it. Most parents would be too chicken to have a 3-year-old near a hot skillet, but I felt this particular activity was person-appropriate for him. He had never colored on the walls, fallen down the steps, or thrown his truck into art work. I assessed that he had good self-control, and that this would be a fabulous–even scientific–teaching opportunity. I got a chair for him to stand on and explained in detail what he and I were going to do. His face looked like your face would look if I told you, "I'm giving you a million dollars, no strings attached."

I went over how hot the stove and skillet were, and told him not to touch it. He got it.

I said, "Let's start by cracking the egg open." I spread a towel on the floor and got the egg carton, a bowl, a paper towel, and a spoon to retrieve any bits of eggshell. I cracked one and then—yes—let him crack one. He had so much fun, we cracked three more. Then I got a fork and showed him how to whip them up. He did it too, to his delight.

Now it was time to cook the eggs. I boosted him up onto the chair and showed him how to hold his hand near the heat, so he could see how hot it was. I put the butter in the skillet, and he relished watching it melt. Next we poured the egg mixture in, and we watched it cook. We held the spatula together. At no time was he in danger, but he was learning to do something that grown-ups do, and he was so delighted. It just opened both of our hearts. He was so proud of eating the eggs that he prepared!

It's a win-win. You each win in self-love, and you create a winning relationship together. Much better than the typical losing relationship, in which the parent rushes to cook the eggs while begging/ordering the child to appear to eat them, wouldn't you agree?

Opportunities for a challenge are around us every minute.

We just have to put on a different set of glasses to see them.

Wash-n-Dry

When my grandson was two, I decided it was a perfect time to make a game of loading the clothes from the washer into the dryer. I would have him stand in front of the open dryer, and I would take one article of clothing out of the washer at a time and hand it to him to put in the dryer. Soon that lost its novelty, so I switched to "accidentally" dropping a piece of laundry on the floor and saying in a funny voice, "Oh, here's another shirt I'm handing you. Ooops!"

He would giggle and giggle and say, "Do it again!"

When he was 2½, I would drop the shirt into his arms, and he would think he'd caught it. He loved that.

By age three, I would do my funny voice and act like I was trying to toss the article of clothing into the dryer, but I would "miss," and it would land on his face: "Oh, this needs to be dried, and this needs drying, and what?! How did that get on your face?!"

We would laugh so hard that he would run every time to help me with the laundry. The challenge of doing something adults do taught him how laundry is done and turned a boring task into fun for both of us. Together, we strengthened our bond.

SPIN CYCLE

If you have any task that you know your child HAS to learn, instead of dreading it, avoiding it and paying for it later, or wishing it could be over with already, be pre-emptive and throw yourself into it. Get into watching the thrill of a child learning. That's what keeps teachers going everywhere.

Parents, after all, must facilitate learning.

You gave birth, and now you teach.

You don't get to whine, "I'm not a good teacher." Tough. You have a child. Teach her and you'll heal yourself. A child has many things to learn--giving up the pacifier, going potty in the toilet, dressing himself, making his bed, tying his shoes, learning his right hand from his left, brushing his teeth, washing his hands, combing his hair—the list goes on endlessly into the teen years of learning to drive a car, dealing with his first love, managing his time, following through, making his own food, managing his money, doing his laundry, etc.

Bring all of these skills up before your child needs them. Tell your child that you have observed that she is ready for a skill and spin it. She will think you are the coolest. Don't wait for her to nag you to teach her how to drive. Start early. Kiddie Cars at the amusement park, bicycles, sitting on your lap behind the wheel of a tractor. Instill in her a respect for moving vehicles, and incorporate discussions about focusing on the task at hand, rather than multi-tasking.

Many parents lose track of these opportunities for connection because they don't have the patience to teach their children. It's always a glass half empty event for these parents. Instead of being irritated that you have to stop your activities to teach your child something, turn it around and look at it as an opportunity to play and have *fun* teaching your child. Your child will look up to you.

WHAT CHALLENGES AREN'T

Challenges are *not* experiences that will cause harm, like letting your child watch a scary movie or two wild animals killing each other on National Geographic when he's not ready for it. Letting your child go to an R-rated slasher movie when she's 15 because you think they're cool (or so *she'll* think *you're* cool) is not a challenge. Nor is letting an 11-year-old operate a chain saw to "make a man out of him." An appropriate challenge might be to introduce wood cutting and let your child watch, but allowing him to engage in an activity where one wrong move is life altering is obviously irresponsible.

A challenge is *not* plying your child with alcohol so she can get used to it.

And challenges are not chores. Chores are chores. Nor are challenges lessons, as in piano or dance lessons. Lessons are lessons. Challenges are exposure to new things, training and experiencing them together.

THE WIDE WORLD OF CHALLENGES

A first big jigsaw puzzle together, a fishing lesson, a hike in the woods learning to read the path markers, taste of sushi and discovering what it is, exploring an art museum, collecting and examining rocks, learning how the vacuum works, playing with everyday objects, celebrating making mistakes because it's information learned, learning how to pet a dog or cat—the world is infinite, and so are the challenges you can do with your child.

And don't just do what *you* know, so that you can be the expert. Share your vulnerable side. It will come in handy down the road when you don't have an explanation for how something is done.

It's okay to admit you don't know something.

If you've never bowled, gone to a baseball game or the library or the swimming pool, eaten Thai or Indian food, or planted a flower, learn how to do something new with your child. Then you can allow space for him to teach you something that he might have a natural skill set for. Reciprocity is key to learning. I learn from my dance students every day.

TAKING CHALLENGES FROM A CHILD

My grandson mastered Lego Xbox in two days at age four. I still can't get out of the first Lego Batman level. But he patted me on the back and said, "Keep trying, and one day you'll get it." How cute is that?! And true, too.

Challenges in the Wide, Wide World

When my grandson was 4, we took a vacation together in the beautiful mountains of North Carolina and decided to go hiking. I had never hiked but had always wanted to. We went to an outdoor sporting goods store and got fitted for the appropriate walking sticks and shoes. I was quite open with my grandson that I had never been hiking. We were on an adventure together. He was totally into it.

The sales people gave us a choice between boots or hiking sandals, in case we would be going through any water. Water was definitely part of our plan. We were taking toy dump trucks and diggers, perfect for playing at the water's edge. We went with the sandals. We talked to locals and decided on the perfect easy trail.

We packed up the backpack, and off we went to the trail. We delighted in everything nature had to offer and greeted other folks on the trail. My grandson pointed out a snail out of his shell on the path, which I would never have noticed. We squatted and studied the slithering creature before placing him back in the woods, away from hiking shoes. Then we found a clear brook that served our need to dig and get in the water a bit.

We continued along the trail and crossed a bridge. Looking off the side, we saw the most pristine and serene sight: an ankle-deep stream of babbling water winding through massive boulders. We ventured off the trail and went under the bridge, where it seemed we had entered an alternate world. Two pale yellow butterflies flitted around us as rays of sun shone through the pine trees. Words can't describe the glory of that moment.

The boulders beckoned us to climb them. Part of me thought, *Wait, he's only four! Should I let him climb?* But it turned out he was a natural. He had it figured out fast and gave me lessons. "Put your walking stick here and lean on it, and then step here, Nani." We played for about 45 minutes before heading back.

If I had had to do something I was an expert at, or had resisted listening to his four-year-old advice, I would have missed out on the beauty of receiving a challenge.

Challenges increase both of your capacities to learn.

You can make your child better at anything he does in life by consistently increasing his ability to learn.

Children who have the capacity to learn are the most successful at mastering the details of dance.

That's one of the wonderful things about teaching dance. We get to see the same children from toddlerhood through high school, and we keep presenting new syllabus steps and encouraging them that they can do it.

Challenges are love in action.

Challenges teach you that when you don't know how to do something, you have the smarts and staying power to figure it out.

Many parents are missing out on all of these opportunities for bonding, learning, and increasing their children's independence.

Skip sitting in front of a TV or computer for hours on end in parallel "time together." Get up and do a challenge. Keep doing challenges with your kids their entire lives. It never gets old for either of you. The reward for both of you is exponentially greater than the challenge itself. It doesn't have to be an entire evening, but a good 45 minute challenge every day will make the love grow stronger.

CHAPTER SEVEN

THE WOUNDED PARENTING STYLES™ AND HOLLOW CHILD BEHAVIORS™

Let's first discuss that each of us has positive and negative personality traits.

> *To think that your child is not picking up your worst traits is equivalent to putting your head in the sand and pretending we don't notice your backside.*

We notice, but more importantly your *child* notices, and he deserves better.

Around the ages of 11-13, children slowly start to adopt some of their parents' worst personality traits, often exemplified by excessive/obsessive behaviors (hoarding, eating to much junk food, smoking); phobias (fear of thunderstorms/spiders/people/dark/etc.); or other bad habits, such as procrastination, lying, not following through, snapping -- as in verbally tearing someone down, etc. If you are savvy and see these behaviors developing, you can nip them in the bud. Of course, it would be ideal if *you* changed first to set a good example, but... *at the very least you can tell your child, "This is my bad habit, and I don't want you to do it. I'm trying to get my act together and stop doing it, too."* Like a mother bird encouraging her baby out of the nest, you can push your children towards wholeness and independence, rather than letting them repeat the same bad personality traits that you know don't work for you and certainly won't work for them.

However, a larger, more insidious problem has invaded your family, and that is what this chapter is about. My notebooks full of observations over the decades have lead to some great insights into the world of parent-child relations, the chief of which is that your parents were wounded by their parents, who were wounded by their parents, and so on back through history. It infects each subsequent generation like an STD—in fact, we could call it PTD: parenting transmitted dysfunction.

> *Each generation enters the world of parenting from a wounded, fractured state.*

Every time a wounded parent is stressed, he will resort to the wounded parenting style he was conditioned to as a result of his childhood. Back in the very old days, families were isolated, and relied solely on the way their parents, relatives, and friends parented—which isn't saying much. In the 1600's, if a student cheated on an exam or his uniform was not right, he was whipped with branches or made to wear an ox yoke all day. One can only imagine what happened at home. This barbaric way of dealing with children has just been passed from one generation to the next, with few changes being made along the way.

Many people are concerned with childhood obesity these days, but little is being said about the super-sized parenting problem among us. Sadly, poor parenting is the norm, because our society does not encourage healthy parenting. The majority of the world has been lulled into a hypnotic state of bad parenting.

We need to recognize that we have an epidemic parenting problem and then muster the courage to care enough to do something about it.

Your new job is to make sure that your dysfunction is not transmitted to your child and future generations.

I've identified seven Wounded Parenting Styles that unintentionally create harmful, fractured, DUBOOs within our children. These wounds cause problems for decades, unless the fracture is healed. These Wounded Parenting Styles give rise to what I call the seven Hollow Child Behaviors. Odds are that you suffer from one of them. As I you read through each parenting style and its accompanying child behavior, remember that parents can fit along a spectrum within a category—some are more intense, while others are less so.

Wounded Parents comes in all shapes, sizes, and disguises: wealthy, poor, or middle class; vegan or meat-eater; atheist, religious, or spiritual; stay at home or go to work; famous or reclusive; male or female. The proof is in the presence or absence of a happy, confident, and curious child with zero recurring emotional issues, who can cooperate with others respectfully.

Many kids fall short of major success in dance and in life because they have to expend so much energy dealing with negative energy at home and its repercussions inside of them. Lou Conte, original artistic director and creator of Hubbard Street Dance Chicago, says, "A safe and secure child can accept corrections in dance class and blossom. An insecure child, whose parents leave them feeling unsafe, reject corrections, thinking they are complaints."

> *Remember, if you observe a problem pattern in your child, that is a problem that needs to be addressed—in you.*

If you find that you're getting creative, coming up with fancy terms to address your child's bad behavior, stop. Do not call bullying "impulse control issues." Do not call your parenting chaos their "ADD." Do not call their homework avoidance "mental retention challenge." Do not say that this method won't work because your child is "too clever." It is like a comedy sketch. In the vain attempt to deflect attention from our poor parenting, we act like Big Pharma, coming up with diagnosable diseases to explain our children's behavior. The alarming rate with which antipsychotics are being prescribed to children is staggering. I say it is all a result of the epidemic of wounded parenting.

Here are the Wounded Parenting Styles that I see every day, all over the world.

> *Read with your eyes wide open—and read each chapter as if it were written for you.*

Really, unless you change out of that awful marigold polyester double breasted suit of toxicity, your child's spirit will be scarred with the destruction you unwittingly model every day. Practice the Hanson Method every day until you embody that healthy parenting style.

"SUPER FREAK" IS ONLY GOOD FOR A SONG TITLE

Does your child routinely come home complaining about teachers at school or dance class? Does he feel that the teacher is too mean, or that she embarrasses him? And do you agree with him, feeling your blood boil because your child is upset, incredulous that the teacher would say or do that to *your* child? Do you just have an urge to get right in there and deal with the teacher? Do you find that as your child gets older, his mouth is getting smarter—and not in a good way? Does he talk back? Does he misbehave right in front of you, knowing he is "gonna get it?" If so, guess what? Your child is what I call a Negative Vortex Child™, and you, I'm afraid (and often I am), are a Super Freak Parent™. Welcome to our first Wounded Parenting Style and resultant Hollow Child Behavior.

SUPER FREAKY

Here's one of many things your child knows, that you don't know that she knows: she knows when you've lost it—when you turn into Super Freak. She knows this at age 4. The bulging eyes, the vein pulsating in your forehead, the barking of orders, the yelling, the throwing, the hitting, the cussing under your breath…yeah, she knows you have become the Super Freak, and she hates it. She doesn't dislike it or find it mildly unpleasant; she hates it.

Truth be told, so do you. You know the aftermath. "Why did I go there?" Followed by, "Maybe she didn't notice. Or won't remember."

Oh, she remembers. She didn't have a night of martinis. Of course she remembers. There were red and green lights flashing behind you, like a Darth Vader light saber convention.

Super Freaks are, at their cores, manic control freaks who need to protect their own insecurities about not being perfect.

This means their children, their mates, their houses, their coworkers—everything in their lives has to uphold the legend of their perfection. They are quick to feel attacked when no attack was ever launched. They will let everyone know what they've taken issue with because they conjured up an intention that wasn't there. This parenting style fosters the growth of what is known as a "stage parent" or "dance mom."

Super Freaks are the scariest-in-public of all the bad parenting models I'll present here. They can come UNGLUED over anything that they want to maintain control over. They will freak out. They will do it in front of anyone, or by email, and it's not pretty. They will destroy anything that might shine a bright light on their sense of imperfection. If destruction is not possible, they will bring out the Double Ds.

DOUBLE DS ARE HARD TO SUPPORT

When someone leads with their double Ds, it's hard not to notice. They put them right in your face and expect you to deal with it.

Denial and Defensiveness. These are the twin traits of the Super Freak that will contaminate their children. And their mates. And their co-workers. And their children's dance teacher.

We've all run into a Super Freak. They are the ones you find yourself shrinking in front of. The counterperson at the post office who takes an unbelievable amount of time to tidy their paper clips rather than wait on you, while you stand there holding a heavy package. The returns clerk who organizes hangers and talks to coworkers about evening plans—anything but assist you. Intuitively, we know we have to shrink, contracting our joy back into ourselves so the Super Freak doesn't feel diminished and attack us or try to lord power over us.

The Double Ds, denial and defensiveness, are the armor of the Super Freaks. They are like porcupines—get too close, and you run the risk that they'll release their quills in your face over the slightest disturbance. You have to walk on eggshells when you're around them.

An Awkward Encounter

I was once at a salon where everyone behaved this way around the manager. She was curt with customers; if she messed up someone's appointment, she would blame it on something—the customer didn't speak loudly enough; there was too much salon noise; a mystery person erased the appointment she'd entered. I asked my hairdresser about her, and he said they had had yelling matches about her recent habit of coming over to stand and stare at clients. I asked if he'd talked to the owner, and he said he had, but the offsite owner didn't believe him. My hairdresser, Derrick, said it was making him angry, and it was stressing out his clients.

It wasn't long before the manager came over and stood and stared at me and Derrick—really stared, with arms crossed. We stopped our conversation, as it was none of her business, and I waited to hear the reason she was there. She didn't say a word for over a minute. She just stood there. Then she just as suddenly left. Later, she came back and did it again.

It was awkward, to say the least. I decided I would say something to her when I settled up my bill. I knew she was a Super Freak, and if she became a problem, I'd have to make a decision whether I wanted to return in the future.

When my hair was done, I stood before the manager's desk, ignoring the desire to shrink. I said, "I felt uncomfortable when you came and stood and stared during my haircut. I'm curious—why did you do that?"

The manager, flabbergasted, said, "I'm sorry if you took it that way. I'm the manager here, and that's what I do."

I asked, "And what exactly is that, staring at me while I'm getting my hair cut?"

She said, "I want to make sure Derrick is okay."

I asked, "'Okay' as in safe from an attacking customer, or able to cut?" She responded, "Well, it's a complicated cut, so I want to make sure he's okay."

One thing about Super Freaks is that they will have an endless list of nonsensical excuses. But if they roll you over, they will come back to take out your soft underbelly of forgiveness, and it will only get worse with their criticism.

I continued, "Oh. Are you a hairdresser? Do you think he's not capable?"

She said, "Well, no."

I said, "Then how do you determine if he's okay doing the cut?"

She was clearly distressed and switched tactics, "I thought I knew you-- that we had a conversation once."

I said, "Oh, I'm sorry. I don't remember you. What was it about?"

She said, "Uh, I think we met at a restaurant, and we were talking."

Now I may forget a few things, but not that. So rather than go a few more rounds listening to excuses I decided to wrap it up. "Oh, the fried chicken place with the gravy on the biscuits on the east side of town?"

"Yes, that was it," she said.

Anyone who knows me knows I would never eat that, and there isn't such a restaurant in our town. I responded, "Then you have me confused with someone else."

She tried to turn the tables one more time, saying, "What do you want me to do? Give blood? I'm sorry."

I said, "I want you to stop coming over and interrupting my haircut."

And that was the end of that. Until...

One day, during my daily updates with my office assistant, she said, "A woman who was—shall we say, annoying?—came to enroll today. I'm not sure if you'll take her."

"What did she do?" I asked.

"Well, she turned in the papers, and the waiver was missing. I said, 'Oh, I'll need a waiver signed,' and I was super polite, too. I guess she thought she had everything together and didn't like a mistake being pointed out or something, maybe—I don't know. But she launched a tirade that went something like this: 'You know what? I don't have time to read all of your ridiculous papers. I'm busy, and you should have them color coded so that you know which one is next, and who has time for this? I work, and I'm a mother, and I don't like the tone of a waiver. I'm a great parent, so maybe I should redo all of your papers so that busy mothers can get through them, because I would never *miss* a paper, and I'm not sure if I want to be somewhere that has a waiver. You know what? I have to rethink this whole thing. I'll get back to you.' And then she stormed out the door."

My assistant handed me the papers, and I asked why they were curled up. She explained that the woman had rolled them up and used them to strike the reception counter for emphasis. I uncurled them and saw the name. It was the manager of the salon.

We didn't take her enrollment when her husband returned with the missing waiver. If someone is difficult during the enrollment process, it's just a matter of time before I dismiss her from the studio.

The Super Freaks' Double Ds are in place so that no one engages them on an authentic level. They get to be power players and run over everyone, often making up absurd reasons that you can't talk to them ("My phone is for emergencies only," or "I'm too busy for a conversation," shortly after they've dumped on you. They are so wounded and so on edge. They cannot take any criticism without producing machete knives for slicing you up and down. Can you imagine being raised by a Double D parent? Ugh!

As you might guess, Super Freaks parent in a chaotic manner. They're extremely volatile; they have an insatiable need to appear as though they have it all together to the world, but then they overflow with denial and defensiveness when they're challenged. They take their children to doctors, and if the doctor doesn't agree with them, they plow ahead and bounce from doctor to doctor until they hear what they like. If necessary, they will find ways to intimidate any professional they're working with—becoming quite indignant, or getting up in someone's face. Most professionals they deal with just say "Whatever," and let them go—which, in some ways, gives the Super Freaks a false sense of power. Super Freaks will go from freaking out on their kids one minute to having in-depth life conversations with them the next. They will be lovey-dovey with their children, and then switch to super-controlling and holding their children back the next. They will give their children a long leash one moment, and then have them tucked into bed way too early the next. The only consistency about Super Freaks is the inconsistency.

Super Freaks have a strong need for control, so they make decisions that will ultimately damage their children's wholeness, but in their minds it's couched in the myth of their own superiority and omniscience. They do things like enroll their child in dance, and then suddenly decide mid-semester that their child can't handle a certain class for some concocted reason—it's too taxing, their child is complaining—whatever. Then, the next semester, the Super Freak will re-enroll the child and add *more* classes! Later they will take it away again. They like to make decisions as though they know what is best in dance for their child, even though they do not have a background to make these decisions with. At some point these same parents will end up telling the dance school, "I don't know if she is clear on what she wants in dance." Gee, I wonder why?

THE CHILDREN OF SUPER FREAKS: THE NEGATIVE VORTEX CHILDREN™

Sometimes kids line up backstage and peer out from behind the curtain, thinking that the audience can't see them, because they can't see the audience sitting beyond the stage in the dark. It's always a shocker to the kids when I inform them we can indeed see them.

And this may be a shocker to you: a dance teacher knows which parents are Super Freaks. Sometimes we know because you freak out at the studio. But a seasoned teacher or coach knows because the children of Super Freaks often experience what I like to characterize as "negative vortex" episodes, in which they go into a tornadic spin that affects everyone around them. These children do not literally spin, of course, but you can see their emotions spiraling out of control, sucking the energy out of the classroom as it goes.

Yes, Negative Vortexes are the offspring of Super Freaks. They can't often spin at home because of the Super Freak's negative energy, so they do it where they feel safe. These children are often either pouty, charged with an "I dare you to correct me" attitude, or they have adopted a "happy hapless mask" to cover up their negative vortex center. They don't do well with lists, requirements, accountability, follow-through, or deadlines. Even the blatantly pouty Negative Vortexes can be very nice, silly, and entertaining; it's just that when they are in one of their moods, they make sure the entire class suffers with them. These children often excel in one area, like dance, but they cannot focus on much in dance class, because they worry about doing things wrong, or they become irritated when others may be doing steps wrong. They huff, they puff, they glare, they stare, and they often look generally ticked off.

Up until about age 8, Negative Vortexes will always raise their hands when I ask, "Who wants to be the best?" But if I ask, "Who wants to work hard?" they will put their hands down. Any little request for improvement can set them off in a downward spiral. Too many corrections on dance steps, not doing something right in class, fear of not getting a brand new step—any of these can trigger a spin, accompanied by a glaring, red face.

Whenever the children of Super Freaks feel that they must climb their towering walls of self-perfection, they go immediately from fine and friendly to Negative Vortex.

Everyone in their wake fears them; the energy is so intense you can feel it.

Their vortexes of negativity are laced with a palpable anger. As they get older, the judging of others and the bullying—verbal or physical—can begin. In their minds they are quick to lash out at others—adults or children. Only upon application of the Six Steps does one discover the darkness of their judgmental thoughts towards their peers and teachers. These are the spinning internal negative thoughts. They become quiet bullies. They put down anyone they perceive as being better than they are and quietly but consistently intimidate them through looks and words. They're just repeating what they have experienced at home. Then they go home and complain to their Super Freak Parents, who send off scathing emails or make dramatic appearances in person.

Negative Vortexes learn all of these characteristics from their Super Freak Parents, who are hard core in the judgment category. These parents are super critical, explosive, and controlling, known to lash out at their children in a sudden attack: "Put the orange juice on the third shelf, not the second. Are you stupid?" "Can't you see that I'm on the phone, you idiot?" "No, don't do that. You don't know how." Super Freaks barely tolerate their kids' flaws, or anyone else's. Spanking is often used as punishment, especially in the early years. The child is always on edge in this abusive relationship, where the Super Freak's word is the law. That's why it's hard for them to focus in dance. They have trained part of their brain to wait for the inevitable bomb. Everyone learns to walk a thin line with these students, for they, too, have become bombs waiting to explode.

Negative Vortexes are often plagued by a host of physical ailments, but they are different from the sudden onset ailments of the Melodramatics (whom we'll get to in a minute). The maladies of some of the Negative Vortexes are ongoing—unless they come up with even better ones. Having been habituated by their parents to an intolerance of imperfection, Negative Vortexes will preemptively create aches or stories to avoid trying new choreography, lest they get it "wrong," in their minds. The Super Freak Parents get behind these ailments, because they can't stand for their children to be less than the best; they have to invest in the fictitious ailments to explain to others why their children aren't top notch. Doctors are perplexed by the malady, which often migrates from area to area, but the parents hunt for one doctor who will agree that there is, in fact, a physical problem. The children end up taking time off of dance; by the time they miss dance enough to want to come back, they are devastated to find that their classmates have advanced. The ailments that these children feel forced into creating get them what they want—a reprieve from the pressure of their Super Freak Parents—but they also rob them of what they want in life.

But these children can also sometimes be complete sweethearts, when their natural state has the opportunity to shine through. It's not too late to reverse the damage done and nurture that part of them back to health.

When your child has moments such as these in dance class on a regular basis, it is likely that you are a Super Freak, or victimizer, and you need to change. Maybe you turn into a Super Freak because you are stressed or experiencing your own negative thoughts. ("My kid isn't like me," "I've put on weight," "We don't have enough money," "My kid makes too many mistakes." "Mrs. Jones drives a nicer car," "My mate may be having an affair.") Maybe you're too overwhelmed by parenting to even attempt to do it well. Whatever the case, you are hurting your child.

Parents have an enormous impact on their kids, and there is not much a dance teacher can do to push the children of Super Freaks up over the great wall of hurt and anger they have internalized, except to enforce acceptable classroom behavior.

> *Negative Vortexes may be great dancers, but they will rarely go the distance of their true potential, unless a) they get help and b) the parent is willing to change.*

The Negative Vortexes are too wounded inside, and there's too much mental chatter. They don't really believe that they are loved or supported, even if they are putting on a good face and seem too cheerful all the time. They can't deal with the anger inside and the hardship of the world.

RAGE AGAINST THE DANCE MACHINE

Here's the other thing that Super Freaks will do at the dance studio. They will get worked up and come and unload on the dance staff. I call this going postal. Children long for a connection to their parents, and the children of Super Freaks figure out the one thing that gets their parents' attention. Sometimes, the hot button is trumping up an incident and crying about it. The parent already feels guilty about not having a healthy connection with her child, and now the Super Freak Parent has a chance to be the hero and right the perceived wrong. The child leaves the classroom fine, but frustrated about not getting a step. He cries upon seeing his Super Freak Parent, because really, he wants the Super Freak's attention—a hug and some assurance that he is doing okay. But he'll take what he can get. And what he can get is the parent unloading a verbal M-16 with a full round of ammo on the unsuspecting teacher. This action is, of course, the same thing that the child encounters every day. I will attest that looking down the proverbial barrel of a Super Freak's raging rant is scary. My heart breaks for their children.

The rages are always about crazy stuff, too. A child showing up an hour early and the door isn't unlocked. The child cries, and the Super Freak Parent comes and unloads a round on the studio owner when she arrives. A student is told by the dance teacher that disrespectful language is not tolerated; the Super Freak Parent calls to demand that the teacher apologize to the child, or they quit. A student is 45 minutes late to class and is asked to sit and observe. Bam! Blowup from the Super Freak Parent. An 11-year-old can't do a new trick in acrobatics after practicing it 8 times—no big deal; it takes time. Super Freak Parent comes to pick her up, sees the tears, and yells at the teacher in front of the class, "What did you DO that made my girl cry?" A student is part of the corps in the ballet production; he cries to his parents that he is better than everyone else and deserves a solo. His parents unload two rounds of ammo at the director, who says that the son is not ready for a solo. They quit.

Super Freaks can be quite lovely and engaging, even downright warm. But as soon as you come back from the water fountain, they just have to blab out some hurtful statement—as though you'd asked. They are your friends, wanting to help one minute, and then attacking you the next, over the way you look, what you eat, how you word your emails, or what you wear. Super Freaks even have the need to control other dancers, telling them what they need to be doing, even though they are not trained dancers.

But here is a story to top all stories, of a Super Freak Parent to the extreme.

Announcing Hurricane Mama Super Freak, Category 5, Arriving in 20 Minutes

A community leader had decided to set up some mini-scholarships at the dance studio for kids who showed talent and needed financial assistance, so she asked applicants to turn in a paper stating why dance was important in their lives. Two days *after* the deadline for the applications, an 11 year old Negative Vortex named Tammy came to me and produced her paper with a great flourish. I asked her if she knew the deadline had been two days earlier.

She said, "Oh, I know, but I was busy, and, well—here it is."

I explained that since the deadline had passed, she was out of the running. She seemed to accept that and left.

As if there were a storm rolling in, I could feel the ions in the air shift. The first sign that hurricane Mama Super Freak would arrive was about 20 minutes later, when the studio phone started ringing. Since it was 8:00 p.m., there was no office staff working, and the two of us who were here were teaching in two different studios. The phone kept ringing. I went to the phone and saw the caller I.D. There it was: Mama Super Freak, parent of Tammy. Tammy had probably gone home frustrated, crying about her paper being late. This could have been a teachable moment, but instead, her Super Freak mother saw only the opportunity for her to play the heroine and to do what she does best: go postal.

The phone rang about 15 more times. Not 15 rings. Fifteen calls, four rings each. Since I don't believe in wasting my time, I'm not going to talk to a Super Freak when they've got their freak on. It's the same as talking into a hurricane. It's smarter for me to take shelter.

Too bad the studio wasn't built with a storm cellar, because suddenly the phone stopped ringing. All of the students knew something odd was going on, especially 20 minutes later, when there was a pounding at the locked lobby door. It kept getting louder and more persistent. Finally, the other teacher came to me because her students were distracted.

We thought surely, as an adult, a professor at a local college, she would not continue to embarrass herself. But no, the world must revolve around Super Freaks when they are freaking. And they must unleash their criticism on someone.

Again, it grew suddenly silent.

Knock, knock, knock. Now she was at the back door. Stalker Mama Super Freak. The other teacher volunteered to go talk to her so that I could teach both classes at the same time, since I knew both syllabuses. She promised to be gone for two minutes. Ten minutes later, I opened the door to the lobby and saw that my teacher was getting nowhere fast. You can't run into a hurricane.

The woman was freaking out that her daughter's two-day-late paper had not been accepted. Did I mention she was a college professor? Do they not have deadlines for their students? Of course they do. She said that her daughter was devastated. Logically, if it meant this much to her, they would have accomplished the task on time in the first place. I told the mom that the meeting was over, and that I'd call her the next day.

Back we went to our classrooms, trying to gather our composure. We were both feeling afraid, but were trying to put on a brave face for the students. We resumed teaching.

Then, my Irish dance students heard a blood curdling scream

coming from the other classroom. A ballet student had seen Hurricane Mama Super Freak storming toward the building out of the darkness to knock on the window pane, unable to wait until the next day to talk.

When the student screamed, the woman ran.

This story seems like an extreme case, but it's just one of many.

How I wish I could get the attention of the Super Freak Parent. Very few will hear any advice, as they can't stand to hear about any of their shortcomings. Super Freaks are caught up in themselves, rather than their children; and they are utterly in denial, often believing they are exceptional parents. I want to save the little spirits in these talented dancers.

Look. See if any of this applies to you. Keep reading. We need your help.

THE LECTURER PARENTS™

Does your young child have babyish or pouty moments when she wants attention? Does she make a big deal about little falls and boo-boos? Does she dramatize events and then get attention from you? Do you find yourself lecturing her for having done something stupid in the hopes that she will finally wake up and do the right thing? If your child is a tween, does she think the world is falling in if she tweaks a muscle or has a cold? Does she act like a pompous queen in response to an invitation to a special opportunity she would love, offering to "consider it and get back to you?" If so, here is the diagnosis: You have a Melodramatic Child™, and you—drum roll please—are a Lecturer. This is the second Wounded Parenting Style and Hollow Child Behavior pair.

Oh the Drama...

Izzy, age 11, was a long time Melodramatic. Knowing what I know now, I wish I had interrupted her pattern of behavior when she was 6, but I allowed it to continue. For many years, I felt I offered dance and not parenting intervention. Now I support the child, and if that means having my face rearranged by a parent, so be it. The Super Freaks are the only ones who will really come after a dance teacher, anyway.

I was observing a jazz class from the hallway, and everyone was dancing full out. I came back about 15 minutes later to set new choreography. When I entered the class, the teacher told me that Izzy was sick to her stomach. Now, of course, that didn't match with what I had seen. But over the years, I had learned that Izzy could at any time trump up an ailment to cover any exposure to new steps. Then, if she was successful at the step, the ailment of the day could go by the wayside. If she felt she wasn't successful—whether she really was or not—she could use the ailment as a reason to sit down.

Sometimes if you just out-drama Melodramatics and give them a bit of attention, they will reset and continue, so I said, "Izzy, I'm so sorry. Gosh, there are 15 minutes left." Then, dramatically, as though she had suffered mortal injuries in hand-to-hand combat, I asked, "Do you think you can carry on?"

Equally dramatically, she said, "Yes. I think I can."

And she did the step just fine.

WHO TOLD YOU LECTURING WORKS?

Whoever convinced you that lecturing works was probably the same person who put a "Kick Me" sign on your back. Do you enjoy getting a lecture at work? It probably doesn't even happen. Do you enjoy getting a lecture from your mate? Of course not. I might go so far as to say we despise lectures.

Lecture events involve a paid speaker who lectures on a particular topic that she is an expert on. Paid lecturers hone their skills to balance fun, wit, entertainment, and "ah-ha" moments delivered in an engaging speech so that you, the audience member, are duly impressed.

Contrast that with dad or mom lecturing at home. There's no

fun, wit, or entertainment—unless you find bulging eyes, popping veins, and the occasional spittle at the corner of the mouth entertaining. Paid lecturers perfect their speech behind the scenes. Lecturer Parents vamp on the spot and go long. They would never be hired back by event producers, and audience surveys would say that the parent shouldn't quit his day job.

That's you. The parent. Even if you are a paid speaker by trade, don't lecture at home. You're boring and redundant; your kids got the point in the first sentence.

LECTURE NOTES

Let's break down lecturing for what it is. It's a lazy, two-for-one non-remedy: You get to blow off steam, in order to intimidate your child into never engaging in the offending behavior again. You're like a whale, spewing all your frustrations out your blowhole, and the one person you can FORCE to listen to your crap is your prisoner—oh, sorry, I mean your child. Would anyone in their right mind listen to you voluntarily? Would you do that to your boss? Uh, no. What gives you the right to do it to your child? Society, I suppose. Your parents, maybe.

Lecturing is ineffective, because there's no two-way communication; it's only you on a soapbox. There's no discovery of why your child did something that you disagree with. Perhaps you didn't teach your child anything of value in the first place. If you had, you wouldn't have to keep giving encore performances of the same lecture ad nauseam. Plus, you're wasting a LOT of time in the process of not teaching anything. And it's not quality time. You're pissed off, partially at your child, because he's requiring you to take the time to teach him something, but also—and even more—at yourself, in part because...

...somewhere deep down, you KNOW you didn't do a good job teaching him the lesson he needed to learn the FIRST time the issue in question arose.

Lecturer parents talk louder and with annoyance, in the hope that the child will think twice to never do it again. Clearly, the parent is not applying any kind of critical thinking to this "technique." All that energy expended, and it doesn't even work. Your child will repeat the behavior, having tuned you out after the first two minutes.

But even worse than the ineffectiveness of lecturing is the damage it does to your child.

Every time you show your child how displeased you are with her every mistake—gesturing dramatically, going on and on, getting in her face—you're sending her the message that you want her to be perfect.

She's not allowed to fail, to experience the natural ebb and flow of learning from her mistakes. No. You want perfection. If you could be on the receiving end of your lecture and really hear how laced with your own crappy feelings it is, you might change.

It should be noted that any Wounded Parenting Style can manifest itself in what seems to be a lecture. The Super Freak, for example, is intensely critical—but in shorter bursts. The Lecturer has a tendency to go on and on ... and on. Even when a child hasn't misbehaved, but has merely asked a simple question, the Lecturer will launch into a diatribe—it might be positively oriented, but it goes on way too long, with much repetition and an air of supremacy. The Super Freak's vibe is different—Super Freaks come across as venomous, rather than condescending.

THE CHILDREN OF LECTURERS:
THE MELODRAMATIC CHILDREN™

This perfectionist bent does not lead to your child's perfection—far from it. Your negative energy sets up camp inside of your child. He feels bad. He feels dumb. Eventually, he feels downtrodden. After all, you took an hour out of your busy life to lecture him, so therefore, he reasons, he must be REALLY stupid. After a while it becomes brainwashing.

All of his faults become magnified in his own eyes, and though he tries and tries to do better, he eventually gives up, realizing the perfection he's aiming for is unattainable.

But he wants to make the lecturing stop, so he cries or creates some physical ailment, knowing that if he were to say anything, he could trigger another 30-minute firestorm of words.

While it's easy for Melodramatics to act like fussy babies way past their baby years, they can also create other ways to achieve the same helplessness, such as coming home and pretending they are confused about the details of a teacher's instruction in math or dance. What they want is for you to rescue them—before you can find fault and start lecturing. They may also manufacture other needs so that you will baby them: bringing them their snacks, taking their shoes off for them because they're exhausted, carrying their dance bags, combing their hair, etc.

Even when he's away from you, your child will begin inventing sudden ailments to avoid trying new things (because he might fail); the internal tapes of your brainwashing—I mean, lecturing—play through his mind all the time. Thus, instead of growing and learning, he stagnates. Once he is in his tweens, he'll also begin talking back—turning the fault-finding back on you.

In dance class, the children who don't have Lecturers as parents get corrections quickly. The Melodramatics can't assimilate a correction, because their lecturing parent has conditioned them to turn off that part of their brains. They simply can't stand to hear one more thing that they are doing is "wrong."

Melodramatics are known for their pouts and their helplessness. Any little injury triggers drama—a paper cut, a run in the tights, a simple fall, a hangnail. If a muscle hurts, or they have a slightly serious body ailment, they carry on as if they were dying. While they sit down to await the arrival of their parental chariots, the other children sort of look at them like, "You're sitting down again because you have your 50th headache, but you were just playing in the hall 10 minutes ago? And this happens every Thursday, and your parents don't find it odd?"

Once at home, the Melodramatics milk ailments for all they're worth, with a back-of-the-hand-to the-forehead performance worthy of Scarlett O'Hara. Melodramatics' parents baby them, because they're between lectures and don't know how else to show tenderness. Eventually, the Melodramatics get bored of the attention and go about being regular kids. But then they make one little, tiny mistake—like taking a piece of chocolate before dinner—and bam! Here comes the hour lecture followed by a cold meal and "Gee, once again, I don't have time to do my homework. I wonder why?"

If a child needs to eat and get to her homework, losing an hour or more for a lecture is such a waste of time. And if the child's grades drop, it will be those same parents who say, "You have to cut back on dancing if your grades are slipping." Ergh.

Even animals in the wild know that when a parent is worked up, they should tread lightly. But the children of Lecturers don't have the option to say, "Enough already," or "I have homework," or "I think you are in your own psychological jam-up." Instead, the kids become trained to resort to helpless baby acts, thus becoming Melodramatics. They are also particularly swayed by their friend's comments about how they dress or what they need to do so that they'll fit in. Melodramatics often grow up to be women who want to be told what to do all the time; they learned to be indecisive as children, since everything they did was wrong.

Bonnie's Blues

I'd noticed in class that if I called on someone else instead of Bonnie, age seven, she would pout. If someone else got a correct answer, she would develop a sudden condition, pouting and saying in a baby voice, "My tummy hurts," or "I feel weak," or "My shoe isn't right."

This had gone on for about 6 months, when one night I over-heard her dad giving her a lecture about something. He wasn't worked up or loud, since he was in public; he was just going on and on, and I could see she didn't like it. I wouldn't either.

The pouty acts continued in class on a regular basis. One night, she was missing from her class, and I found her in the lobby with her mom, who said she didn't have any energy. I looked at Bonnie's face, and I could see that she had the baby look going. Mom was already putting her coat on her to leave.

I interrupted and asked Bonnie to come to my office. I slowed myself down and breathed deeply (*Step #1*), and I cleared my mind. (*Step #2: Stop the flood of old patterns and judgment. Get curious.*) We sat across from each other, and I greeted Bonnie gently (*Step #3: Greet at eye level, in a soft voice*).

"Hey, Bonnie," I began, "Thanks for visiting me. I think you are going to be a really good dancer. I've noticed that there's one thing that might get in your way."

She looked interested.

I continued, "Sometimes, if I don't call on you, or if someone else gets a compliment for doing a good job, I notice that you get sort of a baby or pouty face. Do you know why?" (*Step #4: Inquire candidly and respectfully, and really listen to the answer*).

She said she didn't.

I mused, "I wonder if you do this at home?"

She burst out, "Oh, I do! Babies get attention, because they're helpless. So I have to be a baby."

I lit up and said, "Oh, you are so smart and wise that you figured this out! Now here's what you need to know. Dancers have to be tough and brave. Babies won't make it in dance, because they are little and need to be cared for. I've trained a lot of kids, and I know what it takes," (*Step #5: Discuss the situation with love, and decide on a course of action together*).

Bonnie looked like anything but a baby then. I asked her if she wanted me to open a dialogue with her parents, or if she wanted to handle it. She said she would. Then I walked her to her class. She was completely different in class and the rest of the week. She understood the value of being grown up in dance, and she understood that acting like a baby would only hold her back.

During the next week I reinforced the new behavior whenever I saw her (*Step #6: Follow Up*). She finally told me one night, when it was just the two of us and her dad, that I could tell him about our original conversation. Dad was pleasantly shocked upon hearing the details of our conversation. Bonnie was beaming—no more blues from her at the dance studio.

Izzy in a Tizzy

Four days after the major dramatization described earlier, Izzy fell backwards and banged her head. This was a real accident. After the tears had stopped and we'd checked and she had full range of motion, no swelling, knew what year it was, and that I was 22—which is always my age, I called the parents to inform them.

Izzy alternated between dancing and asking to sit down. While she wasn't dizzy, she *was* in a tizzy, vacillating between carrying on with what she loved, and having the perfect situation for getting attention from her lecturer parents.

When they arrived to pick her up, her account of the fall was *very* dramatic. Later, the mother explained that the weekend had entailed lots of plumping of pillows and trips to get designer ice cream.

While the first situation of the aching tummy was drummed up, the head-banging was not. Anytime anyone hits his head, caution and assessment are important, to make sure there's no concussion. If there's any question, of course medical help is sought. The trouble with the Melodramatics is that they *always* have something going on of a physical nature, and it's easy to dismiss real concerns when they come up. This is another reason Lecturers should cease and desist.

Carter

Carter was an 11-year-old in my Irish dance class. She wanted to do well and loved dance, but she had missed so many classes that she just couldn't keep up. Carter was so intolerant of not being close to the best in her class that she would come up with a sudden stomach ache rather than be patient with herself so she could catch up.

One particular evening, everything was going along well in class. Carter was behind but catching up. Then out of nowhere— the stomachache struck. I asked where and how it hurt; the pain would migrate and manifest in different ways. Of course her stomach didn't hurt. *She* hurt from the parent lectures, and she was overwhelmed.

When I'm in class, I can't do the Six Steps, so we both have to suffer. "Carter, gosh," I said, "You've been gone for so many classes, and I think you're doing great picking this all up. Do you think you can suffer through for 10 more minutes?"

Carter answered through tears, "No, I need my parent to come get me. Please!" You would have thought she was having an attack of appendicitis.

"Puh-lease! I need to go home. Don't. Know. If. I. Can. Make. It," she ground out through gritted teeth. On my way to the phone, I knocked over a stack of CDs, and she laughed hard. The thing about melodramatic actresses is that they had the reputation for not being *great* actresses.

I called Carter's mom and told her that this had to stop. She was missing class too often, and it wasn't fair to Carter or her fellow students. She was overwhelmed.

Carter's dad came and picked her up, and after my class was over, I called her mom back to look into the situation a little more. Sure enough, I discovered what I had suspected: there was lecturing and spanking going on.

I told Carter's mom to stop both, and I briefly explained how lecturing and punishment do more harm than good. I told her to buy my book when it was done.

The mother went on to say that lately Carter had been sullen to the point of not having friends, and when they go get ice cream, if her favorite flavor isn't in stock, she throws a fit and just wants to go home.

Parents, this isn't happy behavior. Children are naturally happy. Carter is reacting to all the stress in the house, including lecturing, as well as the spanking and the yelling. Do you really think that the energy flow in the house doesn't go into a child and have to come out in equally toxic ways?

Your child isn't a magician that can transform your toxicity into positivity.

Unless he is the Buddha child, he is going to suffer. A lot. Yet the parent says, "I just don't know what's gotten into him. I don't know if I can handle it any longer."

Really? Try walking in his shoes.

Melodramatics will push on, but usually by age 12 they want to quit dance. Dance teachers across the world are always bewildered when a child who loves dance suddenly wants to quit. These children convince their parents that they need to do something easier, such as hang out with their friends at the mall, join a school club, or go out for cheerleading. None of those things are as exacting or challenging as dance. They love dance—they just can't reconcile their learned intolerance for their mistakes. If someone does not intervene, they quit. And the Lecturer Parents go along with it, because it gives them the opportunity to be genies coming out of a bottle to grant their children's wishes. They aren't thinking of the big picture, because they don't really consider their children or their learning to be valuable.

If you're a Lecturer, take a look at your own child, and I bet you'll see the same kind of characteristics described in the stories above. And does lecturing get you anything? No.

DON'T LECTURE. TEACH.

If you're upset, use the Two-Way Time-Out. Then work your problems out with the Six Steps. If your child keeps breaking a rule, use that time-out to ask yourself if you've really impressed upon her the value of your rule—say, not playing with knives, or not playing on the roof. During the Six Steps, you need to *teach* her the value of not engaging in the particular misbehavior in question. Teach it, don't harp on it. Be creative. Get out a knife, slice into an orange, and let the juice run out. Explain that that's what could happen to her skin if she plays with knives. Show, don't tell. In the case of the roof, (see, you thought I was being a smart aleck with those examples didn't you?) take an egg, go outside, and explain gravity. Hold up the egg and drop it. Explain how your child's bones would break if she jumps off the roof. This is teaching, instilling in her the value of following your rules. It requires being a little creative.

In dance class, beginning students often forget to point their feet. We could lecture them about it, but that would waste valuable time. We have already explained the ballet aesthetic behind pointing the feet, and we've already shown them how to do it. We may go the extra step and use a video or a photo so they can see it for themselves. After that, if they forget, we remind them verbally, or we get down on the floor and stretch their foot. They know to point, they're trying to point, and in time it happens. At no time would lecturing make a difference, and at no time were they misbehaving.

Lecturers and Super Freaks are just two of the seven Wounded Parents; acting ugly and droning on and on are just two ways we damage our children. Some parents err on the opposite end of the spectrum: by giving in to their children's every whim. Let's see what that looks like, as we explore Wounded Parenting Style number three (and its accompanying Hollow Child Behavior).

CAVING IN TO CHAOS: THE CAVER PARENT™

Do you feel like you spend too much money on things your child wants at a store when you hadn't planned on it? Do you find yourself just hoping that your child will get over his bad mood? When he's in that mood, do you find yourself ingratiating yourself to him, consoling him, trying to talk him down? Do you find yourself agreeing to things that you know aren't right, but you don't know how else to say no without instigating World War III? If so, you are living under a Dictator—your child—and you, dear parent, are a Caver.

At first glance, it might appear that parents who give their child everything are great parents—they just want to give their child the best, right? Far from it. Pull the stage curtain back, and there is a chaotic mess of a show, featuring their child as the prima donna. The parents are the crew members backstage working hard to keep the out-of-control show going.

These parents are Cavers.

There is the likelihood that they are giving in to their child's every demand, placating her either to win her love, or just to get her to be quiet and leave them alone.

Either way, they are objectifying their child. They are not upholding their parental duty to develop their child's character; instead, they're living in fear of her next meltdown. I've seen two-, three-, and four-year-olds completely in charge of their parents. The kids disrespect their parents, ignoring them, defying them, and hitting them—and the parents take it. Eventually, these children figure out that their parents don't respect them, because buying them off through acquiescing to their demands instead of giving them love has disrespect at its core.

As actress Michelle Pfeiffer said, "Like all parents, my husband and I just do the best we can, and hold our breath, and hope we've set aside enough money to pay for our kids' therapy." Is that the best you've got as a parent?

WHY CAVE?

The Caving phenomenon is often a result of something the parents feel guilty about, like working, divorcing, finding parenting their children to be more difficult than they'd expected, or suffering from old childhood wounds. In such cases...

> ...*parents are desperate to win their child's approval, or to unburden themselves from the overwhelming feelings of guilt for not having the family they'd imagined.*

So, they give their child anything she wants, hoping that it is the right thing to do. These parents are right to be concerned about their child's reactions and feelings—but there are much more effective, and much less damaging, ways to handle the situation (think love, stepping up, respect, assertiveness, and communication, for starters). Caving in only amplifies the problems.

Ironically, Cavers are better than decent at following rules themselves. Yet they struggle to enforce rules for their children.

Unfortunately, caving in yields the same disastrous results as lecturing and super freaking: the child becomes damaged, and the parents don't feel good about what they are doing. Again, as you should know by this point in the book—there is a better way.

THE CATCH 22S OF CAVING IN
Caver Parents typically fear that if they don't cave in to their children, they could cause their children harm (or cause their children to harm themselves), so they continue to turn the controls over to their children. But that very decision harms their children.

> *The very love these parents crave is demolished by their own actions, or lack thereof.*

As I've stated, being the "nice" parent gets you nowhere fast. The goal is to be an effective parent. And although it appears that the children want to be in charge, they really don't. In fact, they are pushing their parents to step up by subconsciously creating situations so blatantly crazy or chaotic that the parents will *have* to step up and parent. But alas, they don't. And the cycle continues. Sometimes the Caver Parents may blow up up at their children, but the words dissipate into thin air as soon as they're voiced. These parents are just not confident enough to be enforcers. And not surprisingly, these Caver characteristics give rise to a Hollow Child Behavior.

THE CHILDREN OF CAVERS: THE DICTATOR CHILDREN™
The results of caving in as a parenting (non)method begin to surface at age 2, when you may begin to see what I call "children holding the power ball." Someone in the parent-toddler relationship has to be in charge, to make decisions about the when and where of things like sleeping, eating, bathing, cooperating with the rules of institutions, etc.

When a parent is a Caver, the children are in charge—and they are Dictators, tyrannical, self-absorbed, and entitled.

What they want goes; after all, their parents have sanctioned their actions from the get-go. Dictators are unhealthy adults in the making. A Dictator childhood is often the foundation for those "entitled" adults among us—the ones who get a job and immediately ask for a raise and a corner office, and then exhibit shock upon finding out that they are supposed to actually work. Dictators are usually years behind their peers in terms of emotional maturity; they may have an "I don't need to grow up" vibe that holds them back in life. By the time they are in their late 20s, they can swing from very nice to quite mean to intentionally push on your weak spot. They tend to be contrary for sport.

And what happens if these toddlers don't get their way? There is hell to pay. Screaming, slapping the parent, stomping, and beet red faces. The parents are allowing themselves to be trained by their child to either acquiesce or get the beat-down.

In our 2-year-old Dance Movement class, parents come into the classroom to assist their children. Within 3 minutes, the teacher knows whose parents are Cavers. Not only do these children bolt from their parents, the Caver Parents *let* the child run around and do whatever they want to do. They even smile about it, as though they are watching a coma patient come to life. The teacher says, "Parents, we need to keep our children on our laps for this part of the class," but this reminder falls on deaf ears when it comes to the Cavers.

I used to be bewildered by this. Were they not listening? Were they being rude? Now I know: they simply weren't in charge. It's easier for teachers to go talk to the child and get them to comply, rather than trying to talk to the parents. In fact, it's pointless to even have a Caver Parent in the room.

One might think that surely these parents see that they aren't training their children to follow the teacher's requirements. They *do* see, but they helplessly ignore it. They're caught in a negative pattern that they don't know how to get out of.

Cavers don't like being reminded that they aren't doing their jobs, and they *really* don't like the probable nuclear meltdowns from their Dictator children if they attempt to follow the rules and the child is displeased. They might bounce from daycare to daycare, because the rules are too much.

By kindergarten, Cavers have no choice but to comply with the system—they don't usually have the freedom to hop around from school to school. Thus, by age 5, Dictator Children will sort out that they have to cooperate with authority figures like teachers, but as soon as they get home, they give it to their parents a little bit more. In dance class, they struggle with the rules and don't understand that their focus and cooperation is needed 100% of the time. Their focus slips in and out, depending on what they want to do at any given moment.

By age 10 and beyond, Dictator Children have meltdowns or argue to get what they want. They can pretty much get away with whatever they want in the home. They can throw things, talk hatefully, punch and hit, and break rules. They demand that their parents serve them (and their friends), leave messes and expect their parents to clean them up, and casually drop inquiries that are really thinly-veiled demands: "When are we going to Disney?" or "When are you getting me a new car? And it had better be a nice one." They control their Caver Parents through threats and manipulation. For example, if they don't get the attention they want when they want it, they may threaten to run away, skip school, get pregnant, or injure themselves.

By the time their Dictator Children have reached their teens, the Caver Parents are so entrenched in caving in that they can't stop their own children from bullying them. They fear them too much. Having had few to no rules, responsibilities, and chores, Dictator Children often find high school to be a shocking wake up call. Suddenly, there are teachers with decades under their belts who are treating them more like adults than their junior high teachers did. They won't be charmed and manipulated. The Dictator Children, unable to deal with all of the requirements, rules, and expectations, begin to internally freak out. It's like throwing beginning students into an advanced ballet class. They are ill-prepared and instantly overwhelmed. In junior high, they could charm their teachers, but by freshman year, they have landed on an unfamiliar planet. These children are prone to dropping out of school and turning to drugs or alcohol.

Caver Parents will go out of their way for their Dictator Children, often having bizarre conversations with their children's teachers along the way. The following two stories may seem outlandish to you, but they are true stories. Please remember that you might be laying the foundation for similarly outlandish experiences down the road. If your child is fussy past the age of 2, and you feel helpless in the midst of their demands and temper tantrums, you are a Caver Parent. Read on with your eyes and mind wide open.

Ivory didn't need the tower—she had her parents

Ivory was one of my students years ago, when I was one of those younger teachers who didn't know how to deal with Ivory and her Caver mom, Lorna. Now I would handle things differently, but the story is a good example of the effects of caving in.

Ivory had been with me for several years, cute as could be and a talented dancer. Around 8th grade, though, she started missing classes for other activities that she wanted to do. She would always come back to dance and catch up, but she knew these other activities conflicted with dance when she signed up for them. I kept thinking, *Why is her mom allowing this?*

So I picked up the phone and called Ivory's mother, Lorna.

"Hi. I'm calling to find out when Ivory will return to dance classes. We have our recital coming up, and I hear through the grapevine she's doing a play," I said to Lorna.

She replied, "Oh, that's right—you want us to call in those absences. She'll be out for the next month."

I was at a loss. Ivory had already committed to being in our upcoming performance, and we were planning on her being there. "Lorna, I assume the play requires her to be there, or she doesn't go onstage, right?" I asked.

"Right. And she has the third leading part, and she's so excited!" Lorna replied.

"Well, we need her here, too, and if she has this many absences, she won't be able to continue in our production. It sounds like she has chosen the play over dance," I said.

"Oh, don't you get snippy with me!" she retorted.

I didn't think I had been inflammatory, but in hindsight, I can see Lorna was desperate not to disappoint Ivory. "I wish we could have Ivory in our recital," I replied. "That's what we thought was happening. But she's already missed several weeks, and now I find out she'll be having more absences. It's impossible for her to stay caught up when she's not here. I'm sure you can understand. It's just like the play," I explained, hoping she could understand basic logic.

"I got all of that," she yelled into the phone, "But we paid the money, so you're going to do what we want. When she comes back, you'll catch her up!"

"Lorna, it's not just a matter of Ivory getting the steps. She has to get the steps *and* get them in conjunction with the rest of the cast, and they have to get used to Ivory, too. It's not a solo, it's a group piece. It's not fair to Lorna to walk in weeks behind, nor is it fair to the other dancers. So we'll have to withdraw her from the dance. Whenever she wants to return to class, she may," I said.

"No, no, no, no, no! I will find out from Ivory what she wants to do, and then I'll let you know!" and she hung up on me. Ouch.

Magically, Ivory was in class that night. I told her if she missed again, she could be an understudy, because we had to move on. She missed again, and we moved on.

By age 14, Ivory was bouncing around to other studios, only to find out they had requirements as well. One day, she had arrived for one of my classes, and she was standing around with a group of other students, a packet of pills in her hand. Concerned, I came up behind them and asked, "Ivory, what are those pills?"

Ivory proudly declared, "My pills."

I was thinking, Is she distributing pills to students? How did she get them? I said, "Okay, but what are they?"

Ivory said, "You know. The Pill."

Everyone giggled.

"Oh, *that* pill...The Pill," I said. I felt like a parent whose six-year-old has just asked where babies come from. "So, to clarify, did you find them, or what?" I asked. It never occurred to me that her mom would get a doctor to prescribe them to her.

"Oh, I wanted them. Michelle at school got some, and she told me to just say, 'Oh, I have bad cramps, so I need to get on the Pill,' so I did, and I got them," she informed us.

I can't change what Lorna does, so I simply said, "Ivory, do you think it might be better to leave these at home in the future?"

Sheepishly, she replied, "Yeah, sure. I will." Two weeks later she had a birth control patch to proudly display.

Today I know that requesting the Pill was Ivory's outrageous attempt to wake her parents up and parent her with an "I don't think so." But alas, they didn't. Interestingly, one of her parents was a child psychologist.

By age 15, Ivory had her own apartment where she was allowed to stay whenever she wanted, with the option to return home. I never knew who was in charge of Ivory, so when she enrolled in dance, given her history, she and I agreed that she wouldn't participate in the recitals. Then she could have the freedom that her parents wanted for her.

Ivory was always spinning in life, never engaging in it or seeing her full potential, because without understanding how to follow rules, she spent all of her time finding a way around them. She went through a bout of bulimia in a continued effort to find control. She had no follow-through, and rarely finished what she started. She didn't finish high school, and her parents submitted a petition to get her credit for "life experience." I don't think that Ivory ever felt loved by them.

Mad Maddox

Maddox came to me when he was older to begin modern dance and ballet. I could tell early on that he was a very, very smart and creative person, but extremely damaged.

After I talked to him about missing numerous classes despite his great interest when he did attend class, and his goal to be a professional dancer, I discovered that he had been reared by Caver Parents.

The odds of starting in dance at age 22 and going on to become a professional dancer are slim to none, but there are many other dance-related careers available, if that had been Maddox's passion (choreography, dance reviewer, circus performance, costume design, working for a dance company as support staff, either in the office or on tour, etc.). Unfortunately, children like Maddox—the Dictators—may be very artistic, but they are so unfocused that they are like dreaming humming birds, never landing for long. By age 20, they are more like former dictators of foreign countries, showing signs of age and the public's intolerance for their antics. They've lost the cuteness of youth that was previously a manipulation factor that allowed them to skate through life and around the rules.

When Maddox had been in high school, he had cut class so many times, the detention teacher knew him better than the math teacher did. He had been in trouble with the law numerous times. He smoked, drank, and did drugs. He was quick to talk badly of employers, and had been in and out of jobs. He could also write articles and poetry, do design and cartoons, and was occasionally fun to be around. This is what the 22-year-old Dictator looks like.

I sat with him in my office to talk to him about his life. I believed that he had been born perfect, and that his troubled parents had wired him for self-destruction by caving in to him. I was interested to know if he was aware of the bad parenting I suspected he had received. It was an interesting conversation.

"Hi Maddox," I said. "Hey, I'm writing a book on parenting, and it's my belief that kids who are messed up came by it honestly from their parents. Do you think that, or do you think your parents were cool? I'm just curious if you want to share."

He drawled, "Oh, they were all right, I suppose. They did their thing, and I did mine. I mean, they didn't hold a gun to my head and tell me to skip school or anything. But I guess my smoking came from their incessant chain smoking."

Now the gloves were coming off.

Maddox continued, building to the energy of a runaway train, "Why didn't they give me any chores starting when I was young, and some positive reinforcement to encourage me with my interests? Yeah, I didn't want to play football, DAD. I wanted to cheer. And why did I have to hear about their crappy jobs and their crappy days? Kids are smarter than you think. Give them responsibilities that matter, ways to earn stuff. Force them to read and exercise. Don't just give them TV and video games to appease them. Explain that there are consequences in life. That's your parenting job. Promote family togetherness, like playing a game, not just everyone sitting doing their thing, which for us was drinking and smoking. And then don't come to me, saying you need me to respect you, because you didn't earn it, Mr. and Mrs. Parent. I'm not going to respect a teacher because they say so. I'm going to respect them because they went to college and they're trying to teach me something. Kids are smarter than you think, and parents should create ways for the kid to explain what went wrong."

Whew. Maddox was mad. I said, "I hear you, Maddox. Basically, your parents never parented you, and that's what you always wanted, right?"

He said, "Yeah. I'm all effed up, and I know it. Hopefully I'll pull through it and get it together."

Of course, Maddox continued to struggle. These Dictators rebel against "the system" and attract unbelievable chaos of the mind-boggling kind. Here are a handful of his stories for absences:

- Bike run over by a train—but he didn't know how it had gotten on the tracks
- Woke up in the Emergency Room with a bash to his head and a missing bike.
- Bike number 3 stolen by a group of undesirables, while he was getting a haircut across from the police station
- Bike number 4 found mangled in a pond in his parent's backyard
- Partied with buddies and woke up in another state, with no idea how his parents' car was crashed there, because he hadn't driven it.

This last one was too much. I said, "Maddox, I'm not like other adults. That story is preposterous. You drove it there. It's better to talk straight to me."

"All right. Yeah, I thought I'd take it 'cause they were out of town, and I ended up ditching it because I never got my license," he said.

I asked, "Why didn't you get your license? "

"Because there were these Rules of The Road bullcrap that were bogus, so I wouldn't take the test," he answered.

"So that's why you ride a bike?" I asked.

"Yeah," he said.

"And I'm curious what your parents said about their crashed car when they returned from their trip?" I questioned.

"Oh, we're cool. I made my peace and everything," he said. (Of course. Caving-In parents accept anything.)

"So now that you're an adult, and you have the dream of being a dancer or maybe something artistic, you're going to have to discipline yourself to jump through the hoops to get 'er done, aren't you?" I said, smiling.

"Yeah. That's what I'm realizing every day," he said.

"Cool. Keep on doing it. You're worth it, and the world needs your contribution," I said.

Maddox struggled (and will continue to struggle) to invest energy into creating the same far-fetched events he learned to come up with in high school, in an attempt to get his parents to (or someone—anyone) to put him in his place. The rub is that if someone does get real with these kids, it's so foreign to them that they can't get themselves to cooperate with the basics. This is the damage done to these children. Maddox might live at home, or he might even end up homeless. He'll buck the system as often as he can. Underneath it is a totally sweet, smart, and highly artistic soul.

How did these children end up where they are now? It started early. Here's an example of a two-year-old Dictator Child, who will be headed down the same road, if her parents don't change their ways.

The Pacifier Throw Down

Some parents never use a pacifier, while others use it for a short time to assist babies. What purpose does a pacifier serve for kids once they approach age 2? None. Well, except for the Dictator Children. They use it to show their displeasure, hurling their pacifiers to the floor when their demands are not met. Their overwhelmed Caver Parents act as if it's a lifeline, the only thing that will sooth their savage beast. In reality, it's a direct link to chaos, and once again, Cavers come up with some bizarre excuses to support their methods.

One two-year-old named Aspen used to show up to dance with a pacifier color-coordinated to her leotard, complete with a matching ribbon to attach it to her sweater—lest she lose it and throw a fit.

I observed her mother explaining to her that the dance school didn't allow pacifiers. "Would this be okay with you?" she asked.

Aspen said, "Okay." On the surface, this looks like a parent being respectful, right? Wrong. It was the mom's fear speaking; letting Aspen keep that pacifier was not encouraging her toward independence.

This conversation took place every week, until one day, Aspen was in Dictator mode and said, "NO!" She grabbed the pacifier and plunked it in her mouth. The mom knew the rules, so now she was caught in a bind.

She tried reasoning with Aspen. "Sweetie, they won't let you have it. Mommy will hold it for you, and as soon as you get out of class, you can have it back."

Aspen took the pacifier out of her mouth and hit her mom in the face with it, slobber and all. Then she threw it on the floor and proceeded to bawl because it was on the floor.

Guess what mom did? She picked it up, and because it was "dirty," she produced another pacifier from a stash in her purse and gave it to Aspen. Apparently Aspen's mom was well-trained for the inevitable wailing-induced pacifier drop, since her daughter usually walked around chomping on it like a cigar.

I approached the throwdown and took all the pacifiers, gave them to the mom, and directed her to sit on a bench. I squatted down to address Aspen.

"Aspen, what is the matter?" I inquired.

Aspen, still crying, mumbled some kind of pathetic answer.

I continued firmly, "Oh, Aspen, I don't understand cry talk. You'll have to speak to me like an older person."

She stopped crying and mumbled, "I wan' my pac-ier."

Then she resumed crying, to which I responded, "Actually, I need you to not cry when we talk. That's how talking is done."

"Aspen, do you wish that you did more talking?" I asked.

She said, "Uh huh."

I said, "You are very bright, and one thing I know is that these pacifiers stop children from talking and forming their words well. I think it's time to not be a baby, and then you can develop more words."

I turned to mom and said, "Mom, it's time to have a goodbye ceremony for the pacifiers. They all need to be thrown out. "

The mom's face went from worry to panic. "Oh no, she has to have them, or she won't go to sleep."

I said, "Yes, she will go to sleep. Aspen is mad because she's too old to be babied, and she's rebelling, but you aren't picking up the signals. The pacifier is a babysitter. "

The mom offered up additional protests about needing it to calm her daughter, explaining that without the pacifier she is out of control. She ended with, "I'll have to call my husband to get his permission."

What?!

I said firmly to the mom, "Stop. It's *you* who needs her to calm down, because otherwise *you* lose control—meaning, you have to dig down deep and actually parent her. She is 'wild' because she's being objectified. Treat her with respect. Let her learn to talk. She will be happy. And by the way, let her be the one to throw out the pacifiers, not you."

I turned to Aspen and said, "Aspen, come and find me when you are here next. I want to hear about getting rid of these pacifiers and being a big girl."

She nodded.

They did their bye-bye pacifier ceremony over the recycling bin, and within a month, Aspen went from speaking only a few words to chatting away. She was much happier in this regard, but the Caving Parents kept finding new ways to impede her wholeness and independence.

Dictators and Cavers in Action

One early evening, 15 minutes into a 4-year-old ballet class, I asked the parents to come in so I could show them some of the stretches I do for the children's legs. I demonstrated with a volunteer student, and then it was the parent's turn.

What happened next took me by surprise. Within two seconds, 80% of the students were acting like babies—whining, saying no, hitting their parents. And their Caver Parents were coddling them! Some were stroking their children's hair; a couple were even rocking their children as though they were six months old.

We bailed on the stretching for that class.

The next week, before we went into class, I asked the girls, "Hey, what was up with that baby thing most of you had going on last week?"

They looked both intrigued and stunned, so I got an assistant, and we demonstrated what we had seen.

The girls laughed out loud, seeing their baby antics reenacted for them—it was an eye-opener for them.

I said, "Are we big babies, or big girls? Because babies aren't strong enough to take dance class."

They all proclaimed, "We're big girls."

Then I went to the parents in the next room and explained exactly what I've written here about Caver Parents and their children. They all said that they wanted to try it again, and they promised not to treat their children like babies—an act that only fans the fires of the Dictator Children.

We all gathered in class, and I reviewed with the girls what they had agreed to. I got the parents to agree, as well. And lo and behold, it went beautifully! We got the stretching done, with no baby stuff. I even asked the kids to stretch the parents' legs, to see if the parents were going to cry like babies, and the girls giggled and stretched their parents' legs.

I know that without the Hanson Method in place at home on a daily basis, these kids will revert, but I was able to get their cooperation and make progress with them that quickly—despite their years of training as Dictator Children. My techniques are that revolutionary, and they can work just as quickly and effectively in your home.

> *My fundamental belief is that if the parents change, the children will play right into the healthy behavior in a split second.*

And if you use the Hanson Method consistently, you will get consistent results.

And now on to our fourth Wounded Parent Style and Hollow Child Behavior.

THE MASS MANIPULATOR PARENT™

Do you create legends to get your child to cooperate with your wishes, telling her monsters will come up from the basement if she doesn't eat all of her food? Do you dangle a trip to the swimming pool in front of your child as a prize for doing her chores? Do you tell pitiful stories, claiming you don't think you can live if your child doesn't stay in town or pursue the career you think she should have? If you are at a restaurant and the service is not great, do you find that you try to "be nice" and deal with it as long as possible, only to blow up and say something hurtful, because it just slipped out? If so, you are a Manipulator, and your child is on the fast track to becoming a Perplexed People Pleaser.

Mass Manipulator Parents are easy-going one minute, seeming to going with the flow of life and not paying much attention, and then suddenly, they decide they want something to go the way they want it to go.

> *They don't know how to communicate their needs in a healthy, assertive way, so they manipulate people to get what they want.*

And their parenting is no different. Most of the time, they pay little attention to what their child is doing; then, when they decide they need their child to do or be something (usually based upon their own life experiences), they don't know any other way to get him to do it, other than manipulation, which often takes the form of an endless victim-y ramble. If such subtle manipulation doesn't work ("Gee, if someone would mow the lawn, I'd be so much happier,") they start getting more aggressive ("How are you going to be able to handle college if you can't even handle mowing the lawn?"). The children of Mass Manipulators often succumb to their parents' requests, and these are the kids most likely to become "mama's boys."

Crystal Unclear

Five-year-old Kaliyah usually stayed after dance class to tell me about something that had happened in her kindergarten class, after which she would go play with the toys in the hallway.

On one particular evening, I exited the classroom chatting with Kaliyah, and she made a beeline for the studio toys. Her mother, Crystal, was waiting for us, and she said to Kaliyah, "If you come right now, we will go to Target and get your Hello Kitty shirt."

Kaliyah quickly bypassed the toys, and off they went.

The next day, I saw Kaliyah and Crystal back at the studio. I smiled and said to Kaliyah, "How did you like your Hello Kitty shirt?"

She looked down, sadly.

Crystal explained, "Oh, that. I didn't buy her one. I just said that to get her to keep moving and not play with the toys."

While I was shocked at this behavior, and felt sad for the child, I know that parents do this all the time.

This is Manipulator behavior. Crystal usually let her daughter play with the toys in the hall, but then one day, when Crystal wanted to get going sooner, she dangled a carrot—a carrot she wasn't even planning on letting Kaliyah have—in order to manipulate Kaliyah into doing what she, Crystal, wanted.

This kind of behavior violates *all three* of the Hanson Core Principles. Was the mother parenting while awake? No. She was paying no attention—until she wanted something. But even then, she wasn't parenting at all. She was manipulating. Was she treating

Kaliyah like a person? Clearly, no. She was treating her like the donkey in the carrot metaphor. Crystal needs to realize that it isn't all about her.

Sometimes parents promise their child something related to dance: they sign him up for a class, or take him out of a class, or tell him he can be in a production—when in fact, they never intended to make good on their word. And then what do they do? They turn around and tell *me* to break the news to their child.

Fiona Doesn't Want To Take Ballet

At age 7½, Fiona wasn't quite sold on the idea of ballet. Her mom knew that ballet was foundational and would make all the difference in her training, but she didn't want to deal with Fiona. So she enrolled her in beginning ballet and didn't tell her. She asked me to tell her. I suggested that she do, it but she said, "It will be better coming from you."

I didn't fully endorse this approach, but I decided that maybe it was true that Mom couldn't address the benefits of ballet as well as I could, so I pulled Fiona aside and had a short and easy conversation with her.

"Hi, Fiona. Hey, what do you think of ballet—as in taking a class in it?" I asked.

"Uh…" she replied, "I don't think I like it."

"Is there any reason that you can think of?" I asked.

"It's a little slow," she answered.

"I see," I replied. "A lot of kids think that before they do it. I know you had ballet when you were little, but this is different. This ballet is harder, and it takes a lot of work and effort," I said. "Let me ask you: do you want to be a good dancer?"

"Yes," she replied easily.

"Do you think you can work hard?" I suspected she'd never been put to the test of making her own decision about something that mattered to her.

"I think I can," answered Fiona.

"Okay, then." I said. "Mom has enrolled you in a ballet class for the upcoming semester. I won't lie, it will be a lot of hard work, but it will make you graceful, strong, flexible, and smarter. Do you think you can handle that for a semester?" I asked.

She wasn't enthusiastic, but she said yes.

Two years later, Fiona had shown great promise but was always underachieving. She would hold back and I always had to convince her that she could do a step. It wasn't a diva thing, like "Beg me, give me attention"; it was lack of confidence. I could see that she wanted it, but she was unsure of herself. Over and over, I reminded her, "I don't want to hear 'I can't' in my classroom. Say that you can!'"

When Fiona was ten, she and her parents appeared on my studio doorstep. Her parents said, "We support Fiona's decision to take a break from ballet."

I was shocked. All of my efforts to motivate her to be who she really was—vibrant and confident—were going down the tubes. This was years before I know what I know now, but even then I could see that these were ineffective parents. I felt that Fiona was on the cusp of transitioning to greatness. I pleaded with the parents, showed them videos of bad dancers and good dancers, explaining that Fiona had all the potential to be a great dancer. They were framing their actions as "supporting" their daughter, but really they were avoiding parenting.

They explained that Fiona's break from ballet could be only temporary—that maybe in a year, she would come back. I explained that in ballet, you don't take a year off. That puts you behind your peers, and that's no fun for these kids.

Then I had an epiphany: these parents had already made their poor decision, and I didn't have—back then—the skill set to make them aware of what they were doing. So I just said, "Okay."

Fiona continued with her other classes, just not ballet. It is so frustrating to see a capable child exert less effort than she is capable of. Fiona was reluctant to work hard—and that's what her parents were "supporting"!

As time progressed, I got to know Fiona's parents better, and I realized that they were Manipulators. They would say yes to things, and then later, when they didn't want to do those things anymore (or perhaps had *never* wanted to do them, but hadn't stood up and said no at the outset), they attacked. They were good-hearted people, but they could not see that their behavior kept Fiona from really engaging in life and doing the work. The parents were always allowing themselves to be bumped around by life—the mom, especially, never felt that she could control her life. She confessed that she felt she either had to accept what came her way, or attack.

THE CHILDREN OF MASS MANIPULATORS: THE PERPLEXED PEOPLE-PLEASER CHILDREN™

The Mass Manipulator parenting personality is reflected directly in the children, who come to display the same lack of confidence that their parents model, despite outside encouragement to change.

These children never fully commit in life; they vacillate between working hard and holding themselves down.

They go out of their way to learn what they need to do to progress, and then fight internally to block that necessary action. Why? Because their Mass Manipulator Parents are confused and passive, unable to make healthy decisions for the children, or to communicate what they really want; they often resort to controlling their children through "read-between-the-lines" communication. And that confusion shows up in the child—but with a need to please.

Perplexed People-Pleasers sooner or later switch from being confused in an activity to wanting to please, once they are convinced it's safe to proceed. They are work horses in something like dance, but they will never go the extra mile to be exceptional because their parents don't model that kind of behavior. They have learned to please their Manipulator Parents; they have developed the antennae to detect how to keep out of trouble in the face of their parents' unpredictable behavior. Their Manipulator Parents are too confused to be able to support them. In dance, we have to assure such students that we are not going to pull the rug out from under them, like their parents do. We have to overcome their internal worry and teach them that they can plug into life and steer the ship.

Fiona's Back in Ballet

When Fiona was 12, she decided she wanted to take ballet again, because the lack of it was holding her back. Once again, her parents arrived on my studio doorstep to find out what they could do to get her back in the class that she had been absent from for two years.

I explained, "I'm thrilled that she is returning to ballet. However, she will have to put in the time to catch up, so she'll have to be with the younger kids now."

This fell on deaf ears. Whereas before, the mom had been passive in the face of her daughter's desire to take a break, she now displayed her more aggressive side. "Can't we just pay some money and get her a couple of private lessons, and then she's back with her friends?" she asked.

Feeling like a police offer being offered a bribe, I calmly explained, "We're not a country club. Your money doesn't buy membership to the upper levels. Only work gets you membership. She'll start in Ballet I and put in her time. Her muscles need the work to do the higher level steps, and her mind needs to learn the terminology."

Fiona's mom pushed more, but I stayed firm. She wasn't yelling; she was just making preposterous demands.

Fiona returned to ballet and paid her dues. She doubled up on classes and did everything that was asked of her in class. But doing only what is required of you in class is not enough to be a champion dancer.

I suggested that Fiona participate in an international youth ballet competition, which would require private lessons. Fiona didn't think she had that in her. I said that she did, but her mom once again "supported" Fiona, and the 2:1 vote meant I lost. Now that Fiona is 15, she knows that she, too, lost in that decision.

Today Fiona loves ballet and has done the competition. She has shown clarity and focus under my tutelage—she said it "rubbed off on her." But neither she nor her family can see that their inability to articulate their needs/desires has held Fiona back from being what she could be. As a professional, I know that if Fiona had not deferred to her emotionally frustrated Mass Manipulator Parents, she would have been so much further along in dance. This is why I say the *parents must work in concert with the dance teacher.* A teacher cannot do it alone.

I do life coaching with people—kids and parents, young and old—and it's very effective. But Fiona's mom was not interested; she admitted that she was not ready to give up the insecurities that drive her dysfunctional behavior.

I did work with Fiona, and she made great progress. I got her to say clearly what she did or didn't want. But being around parents uninterested in change reinforces the old, ineffective ways. It will be an uphill battle for her until she is older, or until her parents are truly interested in change.

These Rules—Surely They're Not for Me?

Manipulator Parents often want exceptions to rules, because complying entails too much engagement in life. I have hurdles in place leading up to competitions, to get the parents' attention and train them prior to attending an international ballet competition. Fiona's parents already had two strikes against them regarding these rules; a third would mean she would be withdrawn from the competition by the studio.

Fiona and her parents came in to my office, and we sat down. Her mom was spitting mad. While she had passively agreed to the studio's terms-of-service document by signing it, she had not read it. Now she was trying to blame me for her inaction.

"So, Christine, I know that you have your 'rules,' but this is extreme and ridiculous. I mean, nobody reads this stuff, and Fiona has put in all of this time, and now you are going to throw it all away?" she whined.

I responded, "Let's go back. All of my rules are in black and white. I can't take responsibility for you not reading them—or for you reading them but not understanding them, or for you reading them, understanding them, and not following them. We're adults here. Parents read and comply if they care. I am not throwing anything away. You are."

She responded, "But who has time? I mean, what about a break?"

I said, "You haven't been tossed—yet. You have two infractions over simple stuff. All we ask is that you pay attention to the deadlines and respond to emails with 'confirm' so that we don't have to hunt you down. When you go to this competition, there is no hand-holding. You'd better be prepared. We train you now, so that later you don't blow all of Fiona's months of hard work over something silly. However, if you ignore the rules a third time, she's out."

The mom didn't like this answer, so the dad gave it a try. He said, "I see that rules are important in life, but geez, three strikes you're out is a little harsh, don't you think? How about 12 or 15 strikes, and then you're out?"

I felt like I was talking into the wind, and my words and logic were being blown into another county. I took a deep breath and said, "Actually, I think that three strikes is generous. Two is enough, if you are paying attention and want to cooperate."

Fiona was squirming, because she agreed with me. She tried to explain, "Mommy, Daddy, there are rules, and you can't just get a pass because you want it. You have to follow the rules."

Fiona was starting to get it. You have to put two feet in and do the work. You can't passively acquiesce and then when you decide you don't like it, intimidate someone to make the problem go away.

The father responded, "Well, I know, hon, but we've got two against us, and I'm afraid we'll mess up, and there it all goes."

Do you see the pattern? Just like the Super Freaks, the Lecturers, and the Cavers, the Mass Manipulators think it's all about them. They don't want to have to extend themselves. They want a pass! The gloves came off. It was late, and they were wasting my time and Fiona's.

"Here's the deal. You want a pass on helping your daughter, and that's not going to happen on my watch. She has worked her butt off and has come farther and been more courageous than either one of you. She has jumped through every hoop to be a champion. And you are both sitting here telling me that you can't return an email or get her competition application and payment in on time? Really?! I don't think so. You should be embarrassed to even be having this conversation in front of her or me. And you know what? I'm training her to think like an Olympic Gold medalist. She's doing a dance that is incredibly complex, and she can't hesitate or lose focus for a second, or she gets hurt. So, yes, I think you can muster up the energy to do the right thing. Do you think that the parents of an Olympic kid don't have to be involved? They do. They have to know EVERYTHING, like if there's a drug in the Tylenol that will cause the kid to be disqualified. They have to pay attention. *You* have to pay attention, because like it or not, you have a daughter working like a champion, and you have to be champion parents. So start now. Meeting adjourned," I said and stood up and walked out.

I knew that if I had to have such an obvious conversation with Fiona's parents, I couldn't hold much hope that they would suddenly step up. I told Fiona that I would cc her on all the studio emails so that she could be in charge of her future. She did, so there was never any problem again from her parents.

About 6 weeks later, I got a beautiful message from Fiona's mother. She said that she had adopted my way of doing things, and she felt more energized and productive. She now returned emails and phone calls from friends and family right away. She got things done that needed attention. She said she liked her new self. And the father made a big turnaround as well, asking me proactive questions in an effort to get everything right to support his daughter.

On Fiona's birthday, on the other hand, her father had two restaurants narrowed down. She said which one she wanted to go to—for *her* birthday celebration. He picked the other. So there's still work to be done.

Mass Manipulators are tough, because they are very nice people who just have very ineffective parenting skills, and on the surface they don't see it as a problem. They view their manipulation as "guiding" their children to better decisions. While we all have to facilitate our children's decision-making—encouraging them to eat green vegetables or teaching them how to use the potty—the manipulators take it too far, moving beyond facilitating to controlling. Their children become confused about why their choices are consistently vetoed, and they end up still trying to please their parents to keep the peace. Manipulators even try their manipulative techniques on their child's friends and teachers. And with years of practice under their belts, manipulators often find it takes a lot of energy to change their ways, so they, like many of us, often choose not to.

So far, we have discussed the damage done by four different Wounded Parenting Styles: the Super Freak, the Lecturer, the Caver, and the Mass Manipulator. In the next section, I will discuss two more Wounded Parenting Styles (and their accompanying Hollow Child Behaviors,) both of which display a lack of consistent - if any - connection between parent and child.

DETACHED PARENTS

Detached Parents are just that—detached from their children and their need to parent. This detachment can be related to circumstances such as coma, death, or parental absence—when the parent does not engage with the child (because of jail time, abandonment, or the other parent's abduction of the child, or whatever the situation may be). This kind of detachment is undeniably unhealthy for the child, but it is beyond the scope of this book.

The kind of Detached Parenting I discuss here involves parents who have contact with their children, and over the years I have discovered that there are two types the Detached Parents, with adults clearly falling into one category or the other. Therefore, I assign them different Wounded Parenting "sub genres", which will be discussed in detail in this section.

THE DETACHED CUDDLER™

Question: Are you too caught up in your own adult world? Do you allow drugs, drinking, partying, hanging out with friends, dating, a career in another state, or even long work hours to take up excessive amounts of your time or energy? Do you defer anything that has to do with your child—discipline, questions, emotional issues—to your mate, or back to your child? Does your child serve as his own babysitter? Are you unavailable to meet your child's needs, because your needs come first? Do you ignore her when she says she's scared? Do you take pride in how your child manages without you there? Do you think of your child as a buddy or confidant? Does your child cry when you leave (and I'm talking about older children—toddlers are a different story)? Does he get mad when you come back? Do you like to cuddle with your child and discuss life? Has he given up his friends to stay close to home? Does she tell you that your behavior is okay, and that she understands—only to complain about your antics in her teenage years? Does he act like a little adult for you? If so, you are a Detached Cuddler Parent, and your child is an Emotional Worrier™.

Detached Parents seek escape from their lives, and that includes parenting. Whether these parents seek their solace in alcohol, drugs, partying, gambling, sex, workaholism, fitness fanaticism, co-dependent romantic relationships, or other dysfunctional obsessions, they abandon their children for short or extended periods of time, leaving the parenting to their mates, to the children's grandparents, aunts and uncles, or siblings, or to the children themselves. In fact, Detached Cuddler Parents often depend on their children to take care of the parent, as well.

Detached Cuddler Parents lack a connection with their children because of they are too caught up in activities to soothe their own fractures within. Going out and getting drunk or gambling, for example, trumps a quiet evening at home with the kid.

These parents are so fractured from their own childhoods that they spend the majority of their time seeking out negative energy to heal that fractured, dried up part of their souls.

They know on an intellectual level that they have children, and they sometimes even engage in parenting activities, but they are absent from that scene emotionally much of the time.

After engaging in their negative escapist behaviors, Detached Parents often feel guilty, or needy—they didn't find the solace they were looking for, after all. In this state, they attempt to bond with their children, often making promises or buying them random gifts that their children didn't ask for, don't want, or can't use. Since they have no real connection with their children, they really have no idea what it is their children need. They like their children, but they don't "get" them. When they talk to their children, they are much more likely to engage as a cuddly buddy, providing only the most basic protection and safety measures;

they do not facilitate their children's growth, because they don't know what their children need. They just want to assuage the guilt they feel for having abandoned their children, or they want to use their children as a connection to the real world. They can reappear into the child's life and cover them with kisses and hugs, but even while they are engaging—briefly—with their children, these parents are also irritated at having to spend time away from their escapist obsession.

The children, of course, jump at the chance to bond with their parents, eating up even the most bizarre adult behavior, because it means connection. But at the same time, they can sense the vulnerable neediness emanating from their parents, as well as the underlying annoyance, and they are confused. And, inevitably, these Detached Parents go back to their obsessions, leaving their children with the familiar image of the door closing behind them, and no alternative but to accept this desertion once again. The children are forced to fend for themselves—preparing their own food, and getting themselves to bed or to school. None of the basics—love, care, health, protection, security—are consistently and effectively tended to by the Detached Cuddler.

While it may appear on the surface that the Caver does the same thing as the Detached Cuddler Parent (i.e. doesn't assertively protect the child), it is different. Cavers are engaged in parenting; Detached Parents, on the other hand, engage very little, due to their escapist behaviors.

THE CHILDREN OF DETACHED CUDDLER PARENTS: THE EMOTIONAL WORRIER CHILDREN™

Emotional Worriers are the offspring of the Detached Cuddler Parents. I'm all for pushing a child to independence, but you have to be there to facilitate your child's growth in all other areas, as well. Detached Parents ignore even the basics most of the time; their children have no support at all. Emotional Worriers live in true fear—as do the offspring of many of the other parenting styles. But the parents engaged in the other ineffective parenting styles are at least around. Emotional Worriers are left to their own devices for hours (or months) on end, sometimes not even knowing if their parents are *alive*.

These children are emotional wrecks, consumed with worry—worry for the Detatched Cuddler Parent, and worry for their own safety.

You might think that with such lack of supervision, Emotional Worriers would be wild children. Far from it. Instead, they have a unique sense that they need to stay home to parent their own parents—if they show up again. Many become adept at basic survival skills, having been left to fend for themselves as young as toddlers.

Night Vision

I had finished the last class of the evening, so I gathered my things, locked the door, and got into my car. As I pulled out of the parking lot and started down the street, I recognized one of my students, Tara, walking in the dark. She was eight years old. I pulled up beside her, rolled the window down, and said, "Tara why are you walking? Where's your ride home?"

Tara said matter-of-factly, "They never showed up, so I'll walk home. It's okay, I have a key."

I was shocked. I said, "It's completely dark and cold, and you only have a sweatshirt on. Let's go back to the studio and call your parents."

She said, "That's okay. They said if they weren't there, I should go ahead and walk home."

So I piled her in the car and took her home myself. On the way, I said, "I was wondering why you have a key to your house." Not many third graders have a house key.

She said, "That's so I can get in and not disturb them."

The next day I called her mom, who admitted that she knew it wasn't a good idea to let Tara walk home alone.

Later, I met the mother, and I could smell liquor on her breath. I had my answer.

Observing You

It was observation week in my old studio, which was set up with the parents sitting behind a full glass wall in folding chairs. My class was tapping away, and as I glanced towards the parents, I saw Kelly's parents sort of nodding off. I thought, *They must be really tired,* because with the noise of the taps, it was far from sleepy in there.

Soon, their heads bobbed hanging lower and lower, until boom! The dad hit the deck, and within a minute, the mom followed suit. If they had been sleepy, they would have bounced back up. They were out.

The parents in the chairs around them showed some alarm, but Kelly, a fifth grader, went to her parents quickly, saying, "I just need to push them up against the wall, and they'll be okay." She started to drag her parents to the wall, as the other parents, with darting eyes and silenced gasps, struggled to help her. "Awkward" didn't begin to describe it.

Kelly's parents were both high. I don't see this type of parent much, because they don't usually get involved at a dance studio, either quitting or allowing the non-detached parent to take over and cover for them.

Can you imagine living in young Kelly's world? She not only had to deal with this sort of thing all the time at home, but she was publically embarrassed on the one day that was designed to show-case her. Her parents were so fractured that they just couldn't be there for her.

When Life Gives You Starbucks

Lindy had gone with her mother to another country for the mom's sabbatical. When she returned a year later to my studio, we were all sitting in the lobby chatting. I asked Lindy how her dance lessons and schooling went in the other country. The mom stood by fixing her hair as Lindy said, "I didn't like it very much. At school the teacher would yell curse words at us and hit our hands if we didn't get our tests right."

I was appalled and turned to the mom, who was now studying her nail polish. I said to the mom, "What did you do?"

The mom said, "I didn't know about that," and looked at her watch.

Lindy burst out, "Yes! I told you all the time!"

The mom said, "Well, that's how they do it in other countries."

I said to Lindy, "I bet you were scared."

She said, "Yeah. I don't want to go back there."

The mom said impatiently, "We have to go," and out they went.

A couple of weeks later, Lindy was at an all day dance event, and the parents were bringing in lunches to drop off for their children. Lindy's mom happened to stop in to use the bathroom during her jog. She looked blankly around and said, "We were supposed to bring something?"

The other moms visibly reigned in their incredulousness. One replied, "Yes. It's not a catered event. We have to bring lunch for their break. There were several emails."

The mom turned and went out the door. We assumed she was going to get something for Lindy to eat. As it turned out, she'd gone to continue her jog with her latest boyfriend.

At the break, Lindy was the only one without food. She called her mom, who appeared with five minutes left in the break, irritated that her jog had been interrupted. Lindy was in the bathroom, so the mom shoved her leftover Starbucks coffee from the car and a bag of soup crackers she'd dug out of her purse into the hands of another mother, with the instructions to "feed her daughter" when she got out of the bathroom. She wanted to get back to her jog.

Lindy emerged from the bathroom to the sight of her mother going out the front door. She accepted the pitiful offering from the hall mothers, who were scrounging around for food of more sub-stance. Lindy said nothing.

Detached Cuddler Parents: you have a child. It is time to par-ent. Your child needs you. You can't pretend that your obsessions or insanely long work hours are more important than your child's needs. You may find ways to justify your behavior. You may rally "cheerleaders," such as your parents, to tell you its okay. I'm here to tell you that *it is not okay to leave your child without your true engage-ment, because you're too occupied to notice.* Use the Hanson Method to start to engage with your child at a level that is not about just putting a roof over his head and sending him to school. Children need more support than that. You can do it. You will be his hero. Now let's take a look at the other subgenre of Detached parents.

The Detached Censor Parent™

Are you making sure that you are providing the basics for your child? Having her do chores that you have laid out, making sure she's schooled, fixing her meals, doing her laundry, keeping a clean house? When out and about, is yours the family that is well-mannered and quiet? Do you have an active social calendar with your mate? Do you prefer to talk to your mate at dinner, rather than your children? Are you not into all that touchy/feely, sit-on-my-lap-and-let's-read-a-book stuff? Are your children good in school and almost perfectly behaved, rarely needing discipline? Do you allow them to roam and do their things, while you immerse yourself in your own social calendar? Does your home have the vibe of a quiet library? Do you tell your children they have to pay their own way in life? Do you avoid "shelling out money" for extracurricular activi-ties? If so, you are a Detached Censor Parent, and you're parenting a Time Bomb Child, which we'll discuss in a moment.

Detached Censors can be tough to spot, because in public, they are quite accommodating and social, and their children appear to be nearly perfect. However, if you pay attention, you might feel the need to "have it all together" and "be perfect" around them. The Detached Censor parents often have a busy social calendar, whether it's the country club or bowling league several nights a week. Unlike Detached Cuddlers, the Detached Censors do not indulge in obsessive behavior to deaden the pain of their fractures, so they are consistently present enough to provide food and shelter, and to make sure their children attend school.

Despite their consistent presence, however, Detached Censors are just as disconnected from their children as the Detached Cuddler Parents, but in a completely different way—right in front of their children. They exude a stark air of "please be and appear perfect," and their home environment may feel cold or sterile—not because of its furnishings, but because of the absence of family bonds. Detached Censors hope their children will grow up quickly and leave the house as soon as they turn 18. Getting a job as soon as possible is applauded. Delivering newspapers at age 7? Detached Censors are all for it. They are all for the child's steps toward independence in large doses. They will also hold back as long as possible from spending money on their child for extracurricular activities.

Detached Censor Parents, despite their socialness, most often repress all of their feelings and shy away from physical touch. They have a very hard time consistently (if ever) hugging their children or allowing physical contact of a loving sort. While they do things for their children like bathing and dressing them when they are young, there are no kisses or hugs—and forget snuggling on the couch with popcorn and a movie. Without this nurturing and connection, the children suffer, and the damage mounts over time, often detonating after the children leave home.

The Children of the Detached Censor Parent: The Time Bomb Children™

With a smooth, sleek exterior, these children, like their parents, appear to be society's stereotypical "on-top-of-it" folks. There is an order to their home environments, and these children have mastered the art of being seen and not heard at home. However by high school, they often interject themselves into other people's private conversation with their solutions or opinions to what they eavesdropped in on. The quintessential "know-it-all" they butt in often thinking that they can see the only solution that others are brainstorming. They tend to stay out of trouble, get decent to good grades, do well in activities, go to college, and become high achievers professionally. They also have a puffed up view of themselves as being "everything to everyone" and even though others do not agree, the Time Bomb Child never stops to take notice. They look like they have everything together, and they talk a good game.

In fact, these children have developed a highly effective mask to hide the bomb ticking inside. Their parents' detachment from them has wounded them deeply, and the Time Bomb often goes off when they move away from home. They have a tendency to be quick to party hard, binge drink, flirt like crazy to get dates, experiment with smoking and pot use, etc. They explode on the scene with wild abandon. They begin to have trouble following through, and they become quick to snap if you cross them. In adulthood they are *very* difficult to deal with on a personal level, while keeping their near-perfect shield intact in public. They are most likely to join a church religion, with no idea what it means to them.

Thelma Would Never Have a Louise—Until She Moved Out of the House

Thelma was an exemplary student at my studio. She was only enrolled in two classes, but she was always on time, in uniform, with her hair done and her steps practiced. Her parents were often busy when it was time for a show or studio function; sometimes one parent would be in attendance, but rarely both. They always seemed engaging, but distant—they gave off a king-and-queen vibe.

At one performance, Thelma, a beautiful dancer, slipped and

fell onstage, and I thought to myself, "Her mom is going to have a cow about that." I was right. Thelma never signed up for tap class again—I'm sure her mother couldn't stand the public imperfection.

One time I talked with Thelma in the hallway about signing up for a master class. She said she wouldn't be able to attend, because her parents probably wouldn't want to pay for it. One was a surgeon, so that didn't make sense to me.

Another time, she said she'd have to pass on a master class because she had to babysit her 4-year-old sister and 2-year-old brother while her parents attended a hospital function. Thelma was 8, and one parent drove a Mercedes and the other a BMW. I think they could scrape together some coins to afford a babysitter.

One day, soon after Thelma's sister, Dana, had just turned five, I saw Dana in the dance studio lobby alone. I asked her where her mom was, and she said, "She went home."

Home was 20 minutes away.

I asked Dana, "Did she say why she left you here?"

Dana replied, "She doesn't want to have to wait here until my class."

Dana's class didn't start until over an hour later. Dana just turned five, and she's supposed to provide for herself? Were we to babysit? How's that for detached?

Thelma's mom was engaging, bright, and well dressed, and yet there was an "I'm superior" side to her, mixed with an element of "I'm barely holding it together so don't prod." Classic Detached Censored Parent. Same with her husband. These are the families that are hard to research until you know what to look for.

At age 18, Thelma exemplified the Time Bomb Child. Her Facebook page was one big, wild party, and you could picture her taking off with a Louise for a wild romp; all this after years as a meek, mild-mannered, "perfect" child.

Since Time Bomb Children are so cooperative, it appears that all is well. But these children need attention to their *whole* development. If you are a Detached Censor, you need to physically engage with your children: read them books, initiate hugs, and don't stress about the appearance of your family in public. Your kids *are* good kids, but if you don't change up now and use the Six Steps to Sanity to discover what's going on inside of them, your lack of true intimacy will, like the other Wounded Parenting Styles, yield the very thing you desperately seek to avoid: a damaged child.

So how does one tell the difference between a Time Bomb's surface childhood perfection and a healthy, well-adjusted, and curious child? Look in the mirror. If you're the parent of the healthy child, you invest financially in his passions at the necessary level without restriction, and you spend time with your child to attend to his emotional development. Upon hearing of a class with a master teacher such as in Thelma's story, the healthy child would not have automatically said they wouldn't be able to do it—they would know that they could talk it over with their parents. Plus there are plenty of snuggles, hugs, and kisses to go around.

THE PATCHWORK PARENT™

A few parents manage to cycle through four or five of the six Wounded Parenting Styles presented so far in this chapter on a weekly basis. They move among Super Freak, Lecturer, Caver, Mass Manipulator, Detached Cuddler, and Detached Censor with surprising dexterity. I call these parents Patchwork Parents, and their children are Patchwork Kids™. Their kids, unsurprisingly, may display any of the accompanying Hollow Child Behaviors— Negative Vortex, Melodramatic, Dictator, Perplexed People Pleaser, Emotional Worrier, or Time Bomb—depending on which Wounded Parenting Styles their parents show up with.

Patchwork Kids are faced with the extra challenge and unpredictability of their parents deploying several different ineffective and damaging parenting styles, without rhyme or reason. These children never know what they will get, and they have to endure it all.

Interestingly, some of these kids are most inclined to be influenced by positive role models—be they famous people like Martin Luther King, Jr., or teachers or coaches—who inspire them to break free of the chaotic plights they've been handed in life and do the transformational work necessary to change their life. These are the children you hear of who somehow found a path out of awful upbringings mired in the intense and crazy Patchwork dysfunction at home. These kids have survived and found a way to thrive, although it takes vigilant focus. They deal with internal struggles every day until they have crossed over to transformation, and they find a way to succeed in careers of service to others, in turn becoming positive role models for others.

I WILL SURVIVE…OR MAYBE NOT

All seven Wounded Parenting Styles presented here have one thing in common, besides their ineffectiveness.

These parenting styles fracture your children leaving them with emptiness and DUBOOs (dried-up-bits of ourselves) to frustrate them for decades to come.

Your children grow unable to feel love from you, or from others. Unless they are healed, your children will take this with them into adulthood, and the generational perpetuation of dysfunction will live on.

Kids are survivors. Many can live through the terrible things their parents put them through. But is that what you want for your child? Survival? No. You want your child to *thrive*. And the only way you can make that happen is by leaving the old ways behind, and facilitating your child's growth to wholeness and independence by treating her as a whole person and being awake to her needs.

You can no longer parent by convenience or blindly refusing to change.

Adopt the Hanson Method. Do it now, and give your child what she needs to be amazing. Like a withering plant in dried up soil, if you give it water, fertilizer, sunlight, and attention, it will revive and thrive. It's never too late to undo the damage to your child. Your child might figure out how to help herself, but you can speed up the process and assist her. Unfortunately, too many adult children know they have "issues" but are too entrenched in denial to help themselves out of what I call their Cocoon of CrapTM.

CUTTING THROUGH THE FOG

Parenting is a compound problem. Most adults were subjected to great fractures to their wholeness in childhood; they've had to try to forget their experiences in an attempt to block the pain. But as previously discussed, "trying" is nothing. The pain endures. They often find mates who exacerbate their problems, and they enter into parenthood still reeling from these unexamined childhood experiences. All of this creates a dull fog around their interactions with their children.

This parental fog is so dense, it's hard to see the issues that your child is dealing with. While your child's struggles may be glaring to me, you may still be lost in the fog, so overwhelmed yourself that you can't see more than a couple of inches beyond your own nose.

When you're engulfed in the fog, it's too easy to write off your child's problems.

"Sure, siblings beat on each other." "Sure, my kid cries and whines—that's what kids do." "Sure, my kid has unexplained physical ailments all the time. It's part of growing up." No. These things are *not okay*. None of this happens to children when healthy parenting is going on.

The fog is why few parents pick up a parenting book. It's daunting, like a foreign language—but we have to learn the language of our children. Our own painful wounds occupy us, leaving us to *endure* our children, hoping that they can handle what we dish out while we react to our fractures.

Attempting to cut through the fog is my challenge to you. Re-read this chapter; hold it close so that you can make the words out through the fog. Your child is in here somewhere. Find him, love him, and clear that fog so that you can parent him to amazingness. It's true arrogance to think we can wing it and parent a child without any thoughtful parenting techniques. It's time to stop making it all about us. Raising a child is the most important thing you can do in your life, and it needs focused attention.

ABOUT AMAZIN
TRANSFORMING YOUR CHILD'S LIFE O\

You know what is seldom talked about?
times parenting is just plain difficult. How
really supposed to know what to do in *ever.*
We want our children to turn out happy and
and we want to have done a good job parentii

CHAPTER EIGHT

THE UNIQUELY UNFATHOMABLE THINGS (DANCE) PARENTS DO

Behaving badly in front of your children is never a good idea, but I see it over and over again in dance studios and other extracurricular activities.

Parents, please don't sabotage your child's experience.

I am familiar with dance, so my list below revolves around that particular activity, but feel free to swap out "dance" for anything else…"swimming," "piano lessons," or "sports," as befits your own situation.

THE TOP TEN UNBELIEVABLES

1 Not recognizing that the dance studio is a business that expects payment for services rendered—and that babysitting is *not* one of those services.

2   Dropping their child off late or without required items, or skipping any details, and letting the child deal with the consequences.

3   Complaining to their child—who loves dance—about the teachers, other students, the fees, or dance in general.

4   Asking their child why she spends so much time at dance; asking her to skip classes.

5   Punishing their child by keeping her home from dance class.

6   Not supporting a child who is passionate about dance so that he can succeed. (For example, putting money toward luxury items or another family member before his training, or not letting him take enough classes to achieve his goals.)

7   Thinking that paying more money entitles them to exceptions and special treatment.

8   Instructing the teacher on what their child needs in terms of dance steps, parts, or coaching. (The internet does not know when your daughter should be in pointe shoes.)

9   Chewing out a dance student, teacher, or office staff member in person, on the phone or by email.

10 Blaming the dance teachers for your child's: soreness, not being moved up a level, absences and resulting inability to keep up with peers, poor behavior, disinterest, inability to do a step as well as others, not being the best, tears, frustrations, inflexibility, weight, work ethic, lack of responsibility, time-outs, lack of practice, lack of desire to attend dance, or desire to attend more dance classes. (Really, the list could go on. But you get the picture.)

Dance educators everywhere have pondered this great question: *Why do parents do these things?*

Parents don't go to a dentist and instruct him where to put the instruments in their child's mouth. They don't go over a surgeon's detailed surgical movements with her. They don't hover over a computer tech and ask, "What are you doing with the blue wire?" They do not complain about Muppets and Muppet-related culture to their Elmo-loving child: "That Miss Piggy gets all the attention. And Kermit is klutzy! And why do you like Elmo so much, anyway?" Why would a negative parent attack a dance teacher who is trying to do for the child what the parent never did: truly care and believe in them 100%?

It took me years to realize this, but now I know that...

> ...ALL the unreasonable complaints parents make about dance professionals or programs are the results of their emotions surrounding their own failings in parenting their children.

They have lost all objectivity because of this. Along these lines, when parents come to me, claiming that their children need to be in a higher dance level or have a special part in a performance, I know that such..

> ...presumptuous requests grow out of their desires to live vicariously through their children.

Their children are objects; the parents are only concerned about themselves.

Unfortunately, these parents are so emotionally wrapped up in failing their children, that they let those negative emotions dictate their children's dance future. How sad is that?

Peace Interrupted

I was in the office, talking to my staff, with the door open. A mother popped her head into the office and said, "I'm here for the two/three-year-old class, so I'll just go on in."

I looked at the clock: 5:11 p.m. The class started at 5:00 p.m., and there was a big neon orange "Class Has Started" sign on the door. This mom, who had signed in triplicate her receipt of our On-Time Policy, knew she was late. I found this unacceptable.

I knew what she was going to do—I've seen the same thing time and again over my 25 years in dance education. She was going to throw a fit and get her daughter to cry. But I was one move ahead of her—I wasn't going to let her make her little girl the sacrificial lamb for her upcoming implosion.

I squatted down next to the little girl and said, "Hi, what's your name?"

"Deena," she said.

"Well, Deena, what do you like?"

"Dance!"

"I bet. Now, today, class has already started, so we can't go in and interrupt. But I'll see you next week."

She smiled and said, "Okay."

Now here comes the real two-year-old: the mom.

"Why can't we go in? Doesn't the rule say to be here before 10 minutes after? It's just one minute after that."

I said, "Actually the rule says to be here 10 minutes *early*."

"Oh jeez, crap," she huffed. "Give me a break."

I said, "There is no break. The policy you signed is very clear. I understand how being late can happen—"

"I was out of town with work, and I was running late, and she really wants to take this class. She'll be devastated!" she said.

"Deena is smart," I observed. "She understands." Indeed, Deena was smiling at me.

The mom said, "Well, I was just in Chicago over the weekend, and we went to a dance class, and there were kids coming and going through the whole thing. It's no big deal."

I replied, "To *me* it is a big deal. Other studios can run their business how they want."

Now the mom moved on to tactic number 3. "Well, they're only three or two or whatever the hell age they are. I know it makes a difference for the older ones, but not this age."

I said, "Actually, we are teaching them the right way to prepare for class. It is important."

"Yeah, well, I guess you've got all this big business, so you get to do whatever you want," she snapped. She jerked her child's arm and went to the lobby to vent to the other parents there who had been quietly reading and enjoying the peace. She put their coats on and left.

An hour later, I came out of class to hear that she had called and spent two 20-minute phone sessions railing at the office manager, having apparently come up with a few more arguments on her way home. Her latest tactic—number 4, I believe she was up to now—was to claim that the On-Time Policy must have been buried in tiny print. It's actually a full page document, so that went nowhere. Out came tactic number 5: "Well, someone was five minutes late last week, and I even know who she is!"

"Who was that?" asked my office manager, knowing that no one goes in late.

She sputtered, "What's important about a name?!" Then she said that all of this made her child hysterical. When Deena had been at the studio, she'd been fine the entire time. Of course, listening to all of the mom's chaos at home would cause anyone to get hysterical.

This mother has a history at the studio. She had actually been dismissed from the studio eight months before, because her child had been too out of control in class, and the mom and I had agreed that we'd wait until she was older.

Super Freaking was this mom's parenting style, and super freaking was her mode of engagement when confronted with having dropped the parenting ball. She was flabbergasted at her shortcomings as a parent, and so she tried to blame and attack the studio.

Who can yell louder than an upset toddler? An out of control parent.

One mother—a psychologist by trade, I might add—was such a terror to the office staff that their dealings with her resembled a Saturday Night Live sketch.

At re-enrollment, she loudly stated, "I know that three days a week is required, but we will do one, and you will TAKE IT! This three times a week stuff is a Ponzi scheme. You are capitalists! You will not tell me what to do. I am smarter than that. You will do what I say. I am the customer!" And with that, she slapped her enrollment sheet and her check on the counter and stormed out the door.

The next time we saw her was when she came back about a week later, her returned check in hand, along with the letter I had mailed her, wishing her well at another studio.

She had come to apologize. I told her that her disrespectful tone with the staff had gone on long enough, and I couldn't provide the services she sought. She told me that her daughter really wanted to continue to train, and that she would be more respectful. We gave it another try.

DON'T GET KICKED OUT OF DANCE SCHOOL

A dance studio or school is a private institution—not a public school.

We don't have to let you or your child stay, especially if you are uncooperative.

The same holds true for any paid activity for the education of children. In some situations, a new studio may be desperate for students and put up with poor parental behavior, but a seasoned studio director will end it. Nonsense like that takes dance teachers away from teaching the students, which is their business.

The Squeaky Wheel Gets No Grease

I know an absolutely amazing teacher with a track record to go with it, and he is always dismissing parents. Loves the kid, but the parents get to be more trouble than they're worth. One of his mothers had been difficult for awhile. She would gossip, talk negatively, question the choreography—was it good enough for her daughter? She would request payment extensions or waivers, interrupt the teacher and ask time-wasting questions, and exude jealousy and hatred toward other students. In general, she was annoying. Instead of being grateful that her daughter had the opportunity to work with an outstanding teacher, she had to introduce her own personality shortcomings every week, until nobody in their right mind could take it.

It finally ended when she insinuated that the teacher thought one dancer was better than her daughter, and that he was molding that dancer alone to be the best. He just walked up to her and said, "That's it. Get your bags and your kid, and get out."

For the dancer this was tragic. Even though they lived in a metropolitan city, everyone in the dance community knew that he was the best.

This type of thing happens all the time. Parents don't see the connections their children have to their training, because they're too wrapped up in their own psychological trauma from failing as a parent. They will spend a few years at a slightly less reputable studio, and then quit dance or bounce to another location. I've seen the story repeated over and over for decades.

The bottom line: don't poop where you want to train. Fix your parenting skills. Employ the Hanson Method.

And by the way, don't go pulling your child out of a studio because your nose is bent out of shape over some trivial matter or another. If your child has built a relationship with her teachers, pulling her out is like putting her through a divorce—and she doesn't even get to say goodbye. This shows no respect for your child's feelings at all. Your child will go along with it, because she has no choice. But she won't like it. It will make her feel unsure and uncomfortable—because she knows her training is at the mercy of your whims. Think twice before exiting. Your child's training is more important than feeling smug in the short term.

CHAPTER NINE

THE SECRET

Now you know the Hanson Method, with its three Core Principles, and the Six Steps to Sanity for implementing those principles. To refresh your memory:

THE THREE CORE PRINCIPLES

1   Parenting While Awake
2   Parenting a Child, Not a Prisoner
3   Parenting Shocker: It's Not All About You

THE SIX STEPS TO SANITY

1   Slow – way – down – and – breathe.
2   Stop the flood of old patterns and judgment. Get Curious.
3   Greet your child at eye level, in a soft voice.

4   Inquire candidly and respectfully, and really listen to the answer.
5   Discuss the situation with love, and decide on a course of action together.
6   Follow Up.

Throughout the book, I've given you lots of illustrations of the Six Steps in action, and I've also shown you several examples of what *not* to do. Along the way, I've suggested that many parents don't really like their children.

LIKE VS. LOVE

You like people when you feel a certain personal connection to them because they agree with you and your idea of how things should go in a relationship. If someone operates how we operate, it's very easy to like that person. To like and be liked is what drives our social world. We're so desperate to be liked, there's a button for it on Facebook. "Like" is a badge of approval; if someone likes me, I like myself more.

Love tends to break through a lot of the things that "Like" attaches to in daily life. You may not like a person's fashion sense, political beliefs, or diet; but you can still love that person. Love, many times, is uncontrollable, connected to something higher than us, with a life of its own, independent of our personalities and our fleeting human needs. Love doesn't come about because of what someone does; it comes about because of who that person *is*. Love is unconditional.

If you love your child, you love her regardless of her behavior. You may not like her behavior, but you don't stop loving her because of it.

And if you love your child, and you implement the Hanson Method, pretty soon you will like her, too. That's pretty simple.

Conversely, you may already like your child, because you have somehow manipulated her into doing what you want her to do. You are happy with the results; she is now likeable in your eyes. But here's something that might knock the wind right out of you: *you might like your child—but not actually love her.*

Love transcends "like." Love is what inspires great parenting. Love is the backbone of the Hanson Method. You need to really look deep into yourself—*really* ask yourself: *Do I love my child?* Because if you don't, no parenting method in the world is going to help you.

HOW DO YOU GET TO LOVING YOUR CHILD?

At the beginning of this book, I said that bad parenting was the elephant in our collective living room: no one wants to talk about it, but something has got to be done about it. And to fix your parenting, you have to face up to lots of touchy facts: that you objectify your child, that you're frustrated with him, that you feel stuck with him, that you don't like him, or—even worse—that you don't love him. I'm not out to shame you with these revelations, but they need to be dealt with, or that elephant is just going to keep pooping on the carpet.

But it turns out that that elephant was just a baby. Now we get to the elephant's mama—the REALLY big problem that started it all: *you don't love yourself.* All the spinning in place, the avoidance, the rage, the parenting guilt—all of it is really about not loving yourself.

Not loving ourselves takes us out of our intuitive ability to parent and engage in life, period. It grows out of our childhood decisions and reactions to our parents' actions, and if we continue to parent the way the generations before us have done, we will only perpetuate the cycle.

Start now. Learn to love yourself, so that you can love your children. Learn to love yourself, so that your children will love themselves, too. Learn to love yourself, so that you can parent effectively. Learn to love yourself, so that you can engage in life fully.

HOW DO YOU LEARN TO LOVE YOURSELF?

Not by eating chocolate, buying a yacht, or taking a bubble bath. Not by dating George Clooney or Miss Universe. Not by fitting into your high school jeans.

All the great seers and mystics the world has ever known have one point in common: we come into life, whether we are conscious of it or not, seeking a connection back to where we came from. People have studied, meditated, fasted, traveled, pondered, questioned, analyzed, and practiced letting go in order to find what they were looking for.

I say there is a faster way. You don't have to travel, you don't have to starve yourself, and it costs no money.

Simply spend some time with your child, fall in love with her, and in the process, learn to love yourself.

It's a beautiful puzzle: In order to love your child, you have to love yourself; and the way to loving yourself is through your child. The pieces fit.

Your children are the smartest, most soul-filled spirits on our planet. *Let* them love you. You are loveable. And *you* love *them*— not in return, but because your love spills out.

Truly love your child. Save a couple of lives—his and yours.

CHAPTER TEN

THE MINDSET OF A CHAMPION

A champion, by my long definition, is a person who reaches the highest level of his potential—potential that he may not understand, but perhaps someone such as a teacher or coach sees in him. He makes the necessary alterations from a regular life, knowing that he can't be "normal" (code for average) *and* be exceptional. He has a positive *loving* support system of healthy and effective parents and coaches. He puts in a great deal of time outside of what he is told to do to ensure he is making progress.

THE DANCE OF ONE CHAMPION CHILD

I was in Chicago watching and coaching dance students at a high quality youth dance competition. Parents and teachers were milling about containing their palpable nerves; competitors as young as nine were dealing with all of the excitement and attempting to stay focused. The gentle demeanor of the quiet boys and the stick-thin girls in platter tutus belied their athleticism and their ability to attack onstage.

Russian and English threaded through the air, as hopes ran high for the dancers to execute onstage with the same precision they had shown in rehearsals. Varying abilities characterized this competition, and everything was proceeding as usual—until *she* took the stage.

At age 11, this young girl demonstrated the focus, ability, and execution of an extremely well-trained 17-year-old. She was precise down to the smallest detail, and for us, the audience, *the heaven was in those details*. Time stood still; we did not breathe. An angel was before us. She danced with the strength and confidence of a strong pre-professional, winning the highest award possible.

She repeated this level of excellence at the finals—an international competition, where she performed classical and contemporary solos *flawlessly*. But even more remarkable was her ability to persevere even when her partner fell apart during a pas de deux, nerves and self doubt having gotten to him. In dance, it's the boy's job to showcase the girl, but she managed to keep going and simultaneously get him through the dance, as well. This was possible because she was able to depend on something that had been trained into her: that she was good enough.

In case you're wondering if she was a one act dancer, I can tell you that the following year, in the next age category up (12 – 14-year-olds), she did not dance like a pre-professional. She danced like a *professional*—like a highly skilled 20-year-old. She took the highest awards.

I first saw this girl in a class three years ago, where I watched her dance for about two minutes, and then turned to her mother and said, "She's one in a million." The mother replied nonchalantly, as if I had offered an off-the-cuff remark like, "She's a keeper." "No," I said, "Literally. She's one in a million."

Now, I simply refer to this child as the Michael Jordan of ballet, and others in the industry agree with me. Her parents asked that I not refer to her by name here, because they do not want anyone else giving their daughter further grief for her talent.

So *I* will give some grief—to the people trying to tear town such a talented dancer.

SQUARE DANCE

This girl became one in a million because she worked extremely hard, and, in a rare combination of humility *and* confidence, she acts with grace. She is not clawing and pushing her way to the top. She is not paying anyone off; nor are her parents. Yet the haters of the heroine of our story are many in number.

While it may seem to her family that others are jealous of her talent, they are not. Their problem is with themselves, and their own inability to excel. This girl's talent is not the issue. She was not born this way. No one is. Everyone starts from square one. Some of us are born with a natural tendency toward a particular activity, but even in those cases, the talent must be developed. It's our choice to either stay in square one, or put in the work to get to square two and beyond.

Sometimes we don't advance off of life's square one, because we need direction or coaching. But even when help is available, the vast majority of our society takes the lazy way out and stays right there on square one, and then complains when their desires and dreams over in the other squares are not realized. What kind of example does this set for our children?

You purchased this book to learn how your child could become amazing in dance and in life. Don't attack the very thing that you want for yourself and your child. If you send punishing looks to children doing well in dance, why do you want your child to work hard to be just as amazing? So that some parent can glare at her? It makes no sense! Don't cling to mediocrity and expect the results of a champion. It's absurd.

Champions get to be the best through a synchronized series of dedicated work, both on their own and with a coach—with a whole bunch of positive talk, sacrifice, and loving support thrown in. You can't walk down the champion journey path with one foot firmly planted in square one, or do the bare minimum and get to square two, and then whine about not being in square four.

Square four, by the way, is not titled "Excellence." It is titled "Self-love."

MIRROR, MIRROR

Haters' glares and punishing ways are an expression of their inner self-hate. Sadly, this is the norm for our society. This ballerina-in-the-making is so shining with love that she is like a mirror. People approach and they see *their* internal image reflected back—either self-love or self-hate.

Why do I tell you this story of a nearly flawless ballerina and the people that hate her perfection? Because the same thing happens when adults approach children, even their own. If they are jammed up with their own self-loathing when in the face of the pure love their child embodies, they will see only negativity reflected back at them.

Don't let this happen to you. Use the Hanson Method to get back to loving yourself and your children, and you will be able to support them as they strive for excellence, just like the girl in our story. Hers is a journey we can learn from as adults or as children.

The Steps of a Champion Dancer

Many children start by dancing at home when they are little, and the girl in this story was no different. She danced and twirled around the house so much that when she was three, her mom bought her a dance-along-at-home video. Like most parents, the girl's early passion fell on deaf ears, and her parents did little more about it, other than turn on the VCR.

Her family did not have much money, so the mother told our dancer that the video would have to suffice. The little girl practiced that short video passionately, every day, starting at age 3. She believed she was worth the effort.

Lesson #1

If you want to do something, start doing it. Don't let anything stop you.

When this little dancer was six years old, her parents found out that the Ballet Magnificat was coming to town, and they decided to take her to see it. The little girl was ecstatic, but she had one request: to sit close enough so that she could see the dancers' feet. For most children, the pageantry of the costumes, music, and dance would be so spectacular that they would think of little else. This little girl understood even at her tender age that this was an opportunity to continue her self-training. She would study their feet and apply the lesson at home.

Lesson #2

Be alert to every bit of information and integrate it into your action; don't just say "ah-ha" and walk away.

As I've said, children are the smartest folks I know. I highly encourage getting to know them.

Our girl was so excited to watch the performance. She sat in the second row, on her mother's lap. As the dance progressed, she became fascinated with a girl offstage, whom she could see through the wings. She watched as that dancer went through her steps and prepared. Twisting around, she said to her mother, "Mommy, that is her prayer."

Two women sitting next to them overheard her comment, and they watched our girl following the dancer in the wings with her eyes. After the performance, one of the women approached our girl's mother and asked, "Does she take dance lessons?"

The mother replied, "No. She dances at home to a video."

The woman said, "She needs to be in dance."

The mother answered, "I'm afraid we don't have the money."

The woman said firmly, "She *must* be in dance, for her spirit. Allow me to pay for it."

The mother thought about it. She could see the hope of her daughter's eyes, but she was also concerned about the time it would take to chauffeur her daughter to lessons, because she had another daughter at home to consider, as well. This mother is not atypical. Many parents are concerned about spending money or time on their child's passion. I say, a child who is passionate about something positive has blessed parents indeed.

The woman from church said, "I will come to pick you both up and transport you."

The mother acquiesced, and our girl was on her way to her first dance class. The church woman even paid for her leotard and shoes.

Lesson #3

Sometimes when you take earnest action, the Universe works with you to provide something beyond your imagination.

Now in dance lessons, our girl continued to be inspired. She took everything she learned home and practiced. She stayed after her class to watch the older classes. She advanced quickly compared to the children who just showed up for their lessons and left immediately afterwards.

Lesson #4

Take nothing for granted—you don't know when it will end.

One of the dance teachers was so taken by our dancer's rare achievements, that the teacher began to give her complimentary private lessons at age 7.

Lesson #5

If you live to your highest potential, you inspire others. "Shrinking yourself" does not inspire.

The girl had been walking on her toes for years, so the teacher started her in pointe shoes at age 7. She was pain free and continued to absorb everything she could about dance. She was placed into older classes, because she needed the challenge.

Her mom slowly realized that her daughter was unusual for her age; her dad had known all along that she was unusual for most any age. When the two years of complimentary classes were over, the parents realized they *had* to continue her dance training, even if it meant credit card debt. Their daughter, after all, was going out of her way at home to improve her dance. Now onboard their daughter's passion train, they stepped up as the tender cars, to keep their Little Engine Who Could stoked.

Lesson #6

If you persevere, people will come around to understanding your passion. Don't give up.

Unlike many parents who approach a dance school wanting a discount just because they feel they need one, our girl's parents started doing anything they could to work for the studio to pay for their daughter's training. They cleaned, dusted, scrubbed toilets, built sets, and answered phones. They continue to do so to this day.

Lesson #7

If you support people with your actions, rather than your mouth, they will develop an even stronger desire to succeed. This includes yourself.

The girl has been invited to this year's finals once again, but her family cannot afford the trip, so grandparents will pay for it. She will continue to train at the studio she is now at, which entails commuting *for four hours every week* to a large city, so that she can get the more advanced material she needs.

This girl's parents have been able to successfully calibrate their level of involvement with their daughter. Many parents err toward one end of the spectrum or the other:

1   *Over-involvement:* Vicariously obsessed with their child's dance, these parents prevent their children from doing all the necessary work and sacrifice, because they find fault in their progress, their teachers, and their peers, and they often end up hopping from studio to studio. The children lose sight of their own passion, and they view dance as something they do for their parents. Some dancers can use that as motivation to push on, but they are never happy, and they always burn out at some point.

2   *Under-involvement:* These parents provide financial support for their children's training and attend dance shows, but that is the extent of their involvement. They are disconnected from their children's trials and tribulations, so their children have no emotional support system to depend on.

Neither one works. The children of such parents can progress through the dance system, but they will never go the distance or be their best. As Lou Conte, original artistic director and creator of Hubbard Street Dance Chicago, said, "Dance parents must walk a line of being supportive and avoiding hovering. Let your child make their own mistakes."

Although they haven't read this book, of course, our girl's parents intuitively follow the Core Principles of the Hanson Parenting Method. They are awake to their daughter's needs (*Core Principle #1: Parenting While Awake*), and they treat her like a person, respecting and supporting her passion (*Core Principle #2: Parenting a Child, Not a Prisoner*). Each night, these parents intuitively use the Six Steps to communicate with their daughter when she is frustrated over not getting a step a certain way, or discouraged by another dance mom's negative attitude toward her excellence. Her parents listen and engage with her every night, even if it's during the car ride home from the studio, with mom at the wheel and dad on the cell at home with the girl's sister. They make it work, and they are savvy enough to know that the joy is in their adventure.

This girl's father is not interested in punishment, an attitude he learned not from his own parents, but from the father of a childhood friend. One day, after he and his friend had engaged in a bunch of childish mayhem together, which included destroying a few things, his friend's father sat them down and asked *why* they'd felt the need to destroy things. There was no yelling, no punishment—none of the typical parental responses. That act changed his life, and it's no surprise to me that it aligns perfectly with the Hanson Parenting Method.

As for *Core Principle #3 (Parenting Shocker! It's not about you!)*, any parents who will go scrub studio toilets *know* it's not all about them. In fact, this girl's parents say, "If our child is willing to sacrifice parties, trips, and new clothes, we are willing to sacrifice with her." Her father recognized that life as he imagined it—a family at home together every night—was not going to happen. But instead of clinging to what he wanted, he did what his child needed him to do. To him it was simple: put his child first. Her needs were his needs.

The father said that he remembered hearing about U.S. gymnast Shawn Johnson, who won Olympic gold 2007 and 2008. Her parents mortgaged their house *twice* to pay for her gymnastics classes and private lessons. At the time, our girl's father thought, "That is nuts!" Yet here he is, doing anything and everything to allow his daughter to follow her passion. The whole family sacrifices. Our dancer skips parties and time off, and the family goes without the latest clothes or updates to their house. They haven't taken a vacation in years, and the father gave up his small workshop area to create a dance space for his daughter. But they will tell you that it isn't sacrifice in the big picture. Society places more value on material possessions than the development of a child's passion. But material possessions cannot give you that sense of adventure, that sense of having made a difference in your child's life. That is an experience of joy you can't know until you dive in and experience it.

Lesson #8

If you are positively and appropriately involved in your children's lives, you can support them emotionally, acting as a sounding board for them to process issues as they come up so there is enjoyment of the journey towards a goal.

The girl is aware that her father models humility, wisdom, and availability to her. She values his time and looks forward to their talks. She says that her mother is an ally with whom she can go over the day's ups and downs; her mother motivates her to think inspirationally and keeps her grounded.

While they let their dancing daughter know of their sacrifice, they do it in a way that does not burden her or demean her. It's informational. She is inspired by it, rather than feeling that she has to quit in order to lessen the strain on them (which is what I observe in many families). She is aware and appreciative of what her parents do for her.

Lesson #9

Dance can cultivate a keen sense of awareness of the details, allowing an emotionally supported child to take notice of everything in her life, even the support and modeling of her own parents—and even at the young age of 12.

This girl is a champion because she practices harder than everyone else. She prepares herself. Her life outside of class is filled with dance. She leads, and her parents follow in support, humbly. They follow the rules and make no waves. Despite absurd speculation that the girl has an "in" at the competition, or that the parents' work at the studio garners their daughter lead roles in studio performances (People, have you seen her dance?!), as a family, they remain deferential.

Lesson #10

There are few at the top of the excellence mountain and you can't let that disconnect you from your goal.

There are few people who are so healthy in their pursuit of excellence that they are happy and living with integrity in the process. Our girl will continue, I'm sure, with the same determined focus on being her best. She says that she will not let anyone's antics get in the way of her goals, and given her past staying power, I believe her. However, she is a child learning to dance and be her best. She deserves to have both her parents and her studio stand up for her.

I learned the hard way long ago as a studio owner that the DUBOOs of children and parents come with the territory of teaching dance. I'm a stickler that peace needs to be maintained in order to teach dance, and you have to nip uncooperative behaviors in the bud as soon as you hear about them.

Our girl went from being the example of what to do in class, to teachers feeling they had to ignore her in order to keep from upsetting the other students. Nuts, I say! What they need to do is *go talk to those kids*. They shouldn't be allowed to hijack a classroom. By now you know that with my methods, it's easy. Having talked to many a bully child, I know that they don't *like* being jealous. They want to stop. They just need a little help getting there.

TAKEAWAYS: THINGS PARENTS CAN DO TO SUPPORT THEIR CHILDREN TO AMAZINGNESS

1   Venture out of your comfort zone. Realize that how other families around you do things is not going to get you to amazing (unless they have a champion child). Mediocrity is comforting; self-love is thrilling. You will have to go against the grain.

2   Support your child emotionally. Go to the studio or the location of your child's extracurricular activity and see what your child is learning—not to judge; just to see and support. Remember *Core Principle #2: Parenting a Child, Not a Prisoner.*

3   Use the Hanson Method and do the Six Steps after dance classes to set the stage for healthy communication.

4   Teach your child there is value in working hard toward something that she is passionate about; support her efforts to practice. Get to the studio at least 45 minutes early so she can practice before class, and create a space at home for her to practice, too. This skill will pay off in all other areas of her life. It's an investment in her "self library" (a combination of her self-worth, self-confidence, self-esteem, self-control, self-expression, self-value, etc.).

5   Support your child financially. You can always find the money to support your child in dance, if you make it a priority. Remember *Core Principle #3: Parenting Shocker! It's not about you!*

6   Teach your child to value dance not as a social opportunity, but as a vehicle for the pursuit of her passion and developing life skills.

7   Listen. Support your child's dreams. But don't live it for him.

8   Have the courage to stay away from negative people. Remember *Core Principle #1: Parenting while awake.*

9   Cooperate with teachers and studio rules.

10   Remember: becoming amazing is a journey, not a destination.

Just like our society does not encourage great parenting, neither does it encourage the pursuit of your highest potential—unless monetary gain is guaranteed. Dance does not guarantee a high income, so many parents don't support it. "Be a doctor," they advise, as if money trumps passion and happiness. It's sad to see the parents of a child passionate about dance refuse to support it, because they didn't dance as a child and know nothing about it.

Fabrice Lemire, artistic director of Cirque du Soleil Quidam and former ballet dancer at the Paris Opera, says, "If a child has a passion for dance, the parent HAS to follow their lead. Go on the adventure. The parent has to be in the passenger seat, and once in awhile it's good for the parent to get out of the car. Ballet is not by rote, like many things parents think are important—like 'go to college, then get married.' ... Ballet for a child will make the parent grow, too."

Dance students working towards becoming champions are learning skills that will translate to excellence throughout their lives. That alone will put them ahead of the majority of adults. When you are 60 years old, do you want to know that you supported an amazing child who turned into an amazing adult? Or will you have taken the easy-way-out, same-old parenting road? Any of us can advance from square one. It takes one person to break the generational damage to the children in your family tree.

CHAPTER ELEVEN

THE TRUTH ABOUT AMAZING KIDS

Now you know. Amazing kids (and dancers) are born amazing. Each child has the opportunity to continue to blossom in life. But in order to *stay* amazing, they have to have amazing parents.

Are you up for the challenge?

You can do it. Now you have a manual—the Hanson Parenting Method—for raising whole and independent children, by treating them as persons worthy of respect, being awake to their needs, and avoiding punishment.

THE HANSON CORE PRINCIPLES

1 Parenting While Awake
2 Parenting a Child, Not a Prisoner
3 Parenting Shocker! It's Not About You

Most people agree that parents are responsible for providing for some basics: health, safety, and education.

Now you know that you also need to love yourself, so that you can love your child and be appropriately involved in his life to support him mentally, emotionally, and financially.

YOUR PARENTING TOOLBOX

You know that in order to raise an amazing dance child, you need to teach her the appropriate ways to behave as a member of society. And now you can do that, because you have 3 tools in your parenting toolbox to deal with less-than-stellar behavior:

1   The Quick Reprimand, to nip inappropriate behavior in the bud;
2   The Two-Way Time Out, to deal with unacceptable behavior when you both need to cool off;
3   The Six Steps To Sanity, to deal with everything else—to discover why your child chose problem behavior and avoid the issue in the future, and to develop open communication lines to address issues as they develop daily for either of you:
    *   Slow – way – down – and – breathe.
    *   Stop the flood of old patterns and judgment. Get curious.
    *   Greet at eye level, in a soft voice.
    *   Inquire candidly and respectfully, and really listen to the answer.
    *   Discuss with love, and decide on a course of action together.
    *   Follow up.

These are straightforward and revolutionary techniques. The Hanson Method will get you to the heart of the matter quickly, so that you can learn and facilitate, rather than punish, which smashes your child's self worth, as well as yours.

1   Choose love instead of resentment.
2   Inspire instead of intimidate.
3   Respect instead of restrict.

4   Believe in your child. Find the courage to believe in yourself.
5   Don't be your child's best friend; be dependable.
6   As you do unto your child, you do unto yourself.

I'm here to say that…

> *… the more you throw yourself into raising a whole and independent child who you treat as a human being, the more quality time you will have and you will free up your time.*

Just think about it: peace, cooperation, politeness, love—and no recurring bad moods—for both of you. All of that is yours—if you change. It takes courage to want to change. You'll have to go against the grain of society, because we have too many damaged, clueless, entitled, and lost children/adults. I don't hold out hope for the parents who truly don't care. But caring parents everywhere, it's time to stand up, think, and be bold. Be your child's hero. Effect change. You can do this.

And by the way, don't try to pin your child's problems on your mate's parenting style. I absolutely promise you that you are involved too. Both of you need to implement the Hanson Method. It's important that you both support your child *equally*.

Write out cheat sheets of the Hanson Parenting Method and put them all around the house, the car, in purses, wallets, etc. Have them ready. Practice like a dancer learning steps. Put in the extra time. As I tell my students, "Practice makes better." Your child is worth it. Now, go teach the Hanson Methods to someone else—a friend or a sibling. We only master what we can teach. And let me emphasize again: make sure that *both* parents read this book. Both parents need to interact in a healthy way with their child, whether the parents are married, separated, or divorced. It's all about the child.

A FINAL NOTE

While I was in New York City in 2011, I saw a brilliant performance artist named Daniel Beaty. During his outstanding show, he said many profound things, such as "Purpose is the bridge past ego." One line in particular resonated with me, and in many ways was an inspiration to me to transform my notes into this book. It now sits as a sign on my desk. I leave you with that line as a daily motivator to make a difference in your parenting:

The children are watching

ABOUT THE AUTHOR,
CHRISTINE RICH HANSON

In third grade I wrote that when I grew up I wanted to be a "Dance Teacher, Nurse, and a Babysitter." I did the babysitter part early. Younger children always gathered round me wherever I went in hopes I would entertain them or orchestrate something inspiring for all of us to do. I next jumped in with the dance part. I started dance at age 9, and at age 10 I remember watching the P.E. teacher struggle with setting choreography for a school play so I told her I would redo it all, and I did, successfully teaching the fourth through sixth graders dance movement. It was interesting I stepped up like that, but this is how I live my life … I go with the flow of what comes to me. Now, I understand that kids are quite capable given the opportunity so I like to think that the P.E. teacher was ahead of her time.

I continued my dance education and as an adult I danced on TV award shows before I went on to be a dance teacher, multi-awarded choreographer, and successful studio owner to thousands of children. Little did I know that through the years of dance my notes about families would lead me to this book.

Along the way I was fortunate to do a bit of everything. I modeled and acted in film, TV, infomercials and HBO shows. I've accumulated lots of funny stories during this time period and met lots of celebrities. Instead of *always* waitressing or cleaning houses, I worked as the coordinator and event planner for a charity at UCLA. I remember dealing with the Secret Service for one event and walking with the President's delightful wife, Nancy Reagan throughout the evening. Talking with her, and once running into Michael Jackson, were highlights. I had some sort of thing about running into music stars by the way; Mick Jagger accidentally crashed into me when I was 16 and after our tumble, I remember looking up at the biggest lips I've ever seen as he laid upon me and we tried to collect our wits.

Shortly after deciding to leave the acting world, I found myself suddenly with the ability to invent products. I had no idea at the time where this ability came from but I took up looking at machine books and taking meetings with engineers. I hold two U.S. patents for fitness products. I licensed two products to manufacturers and appeared numerous times on QVC as a spokesperson. During this time I had my dance studio business and was juggling my teaching schedule. I soon grew tired of the airplanes (those were the days they were allowed to leave you on the tarmac for hours without explanation) so I focused on building my dance studio. I became fascinated with professional choreography and enjoyed putting dance works up on the same Chicago stages as Joffrey Ballet and Hubbard Street Dance Chicago.

I earned a reputation in the dance industry for being able to take dance students from other studios (who had given up on themselves or their teachers had given them the boot) and resuscitate life back into them through choreography to advance them in dance. And this is where the nursing dream from third grade started to kick in. Wikipedia describes nursing as "a profession focused on the care of individuals so they may attain or recover optimal health and quality of life."

Now, with this book, I can extend a nursing reach to help many children and parents improve their quality of life. I have a strong passion for adjusting the difficult dynamics between children and their parents, for I believe our world is crippled when that primary relationship is not healthy. The conditioning we have all received limits children and adults. I invite you to join me on this journey of exploration and the potential for radical improvement in your heart, mind and life.

To continue the conversation visit
www.ChristineRichHanson.com

www.ingramcontent.com/pod-product-compliance
Lightning Source LLC
Chambersburg PA
CBHW060023100426

42740CB00010B/1573